Retro Graphics

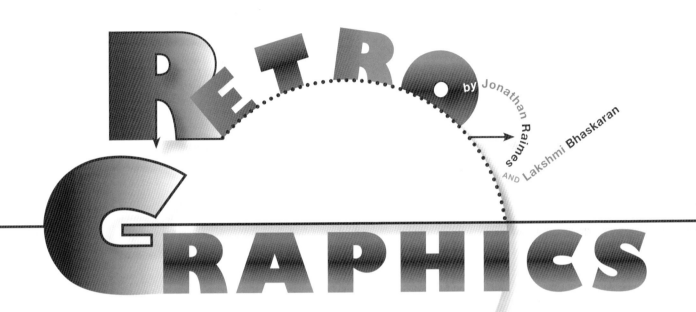

RETRO GRAPHICS

by Jonathan Raimes AND Lakshmi Bhaskaran

a visual sourcebook to

100 years of graphic design

CHRONICLE BOOKS

SAN FRANCISCO

First published in the United States in 2007 by Chronicle Books LLC.
First published in the United Kingdom in 2007 by The Ilex Press Ltd.

Copyright © 2007 by The Ilex Press Ltd.

This book was conceived, designed, and produced by Ilex, Cambridge, U.K.

Library of Congress Cataloging-in-Publication Data available.

ISBN-10: 0-8118-5508-2
ISBN-13: 978-08118-5508-2

Manufactured in China.

Designer: Jon Raimes
Editor: Ben Renow-Clarke

Distributed in Canada by Raincoast Books
9050 Shaughnessy Street
Vancouver, British Columbia V6P 6E5

10 9 8 7 6 5 4 3 2 1

Chronicle Books LLC
680 Second Street
San Francisco, California 94107

www.chroniclebooks.com

CONTENTS

INTRODUCTION

"Images also help me find and realize ideas. I look at hundreds of very different, contrasting images and I pinch details from them, rather like people who eat from other people's plates." *Francis Bacon*

"After some time passed in studying—and even imitating—the works of others, I would recommend the student to endeavor to be original, and to remember that originality should not be undiscovered plagiarism." *H P (Henry Peach) Robinson*

The role of the graphic designer is to organize and communicate messages; to announce or publicize a product or idea in the most effective way. By manipulating visual forms in an appropriate style, the designer can signal that a certain message is intended for a specific audience.

A key source of inspiration in our constant search for originality is the past. Over the last one hundred years, original creative thought has been provided by free-thinking artists and designers who fundamentally shape the way we perceive the evolution of style and the representation of any snapshot of any given moment in time.

To achieve a successful blend of old and new, an understanding of when and where the source of the inspiration is derived is essential. The design "timeline" covering the last century (see pages 10-11) tells a fascinating story. The stylistic movements often inspired one another, or were founded as a rejection of what had gone before. From the Victorian era to the present day, graphic design has evolved in numerous ways. The stimuli that galvanized its development are as varied as the styles themselves; political, aesthetic, commercial and industrial, moral and philosophical foundations—all played a motivating role.

This book attempts to combine inspiration, historical relevance, and practical guidance for the digital graphic designer. Organized in chronological order, examples of the styles and movements from the past hundred years are dissected and digitally reassembled, focusing on the key influences and tastes of the day, while at the same time identifying and isolating each separate ingredient that contributed to the whole. Historical perspective is also added by providing insight into the movements' background, plus information on their major exponents.

HOW TO USE THIS BOOK

This book is designed both to put the various graphical styles of the last century into historical context, and to show you how the styles can be reproduced and repurposed to create your own modern designs. There are two main categories of page that equate to the two main intentions of this book. Both types of page are also tied in with the "Movements and Styles" timeline on pages 10-11. As a source book, you can dip into this volume to find illustrated reference material for a particular style, or you can use the color-coded timeline to see which styles overlapped and refer to the corresponding pages to see how they influenced one another.

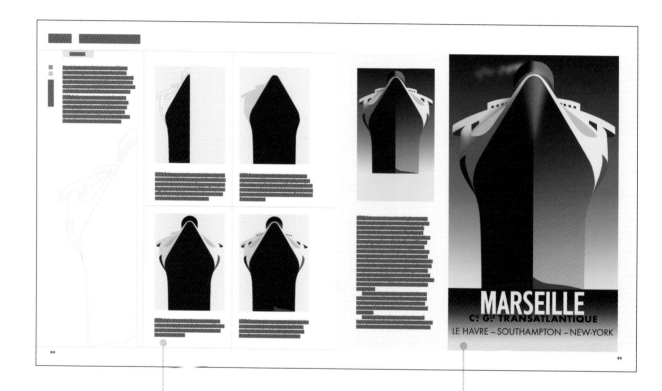

The Method section gives you step-by-step instructions on how to recreate the styles featured in the book. The workthroughs are written using Adobe's Photoshop and Illustrator software, but the techniques can be easily transferred to your favored software package.

The finished image. Full specifications are given for the colors, illustration styles, and fonts required to create a picture which references a particular style.

The color bars at the side of each spread correspond to the colors on the timeline on pages 10-11. They offer a quick visual reference of when each style was popular and how long it lasted, allowing you to make connections between concurrent styles.

The Color section shows which colors were prevalent in each style, allowing you to tailor your palette to create an authentic image. The CMYK breakdown is given for each color for absolute accuracy.

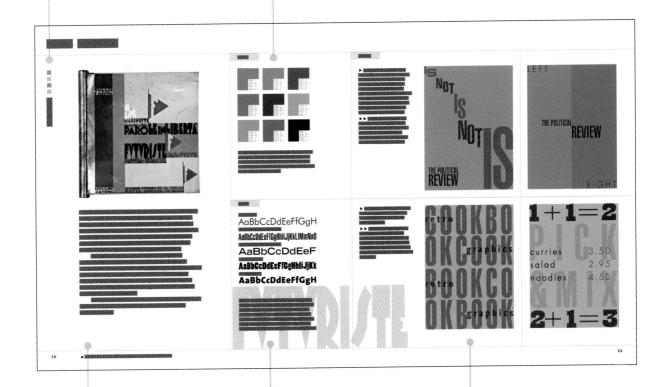

The introductory text puts the style in context, detailing notable features of the style as well as key exponents and artworks.

The Fonts section shows which modern fonts you can use to recreate the look of a particular style. The full name, including the foundry, where relevant, is given to allow you to quickly track them down.

The Layout section illustrates key layout styles from each movement, detailing how they were created and the factors you need to bear in mind when producing modern variations of these retro styles.

MOVEMENTS AND STYLES

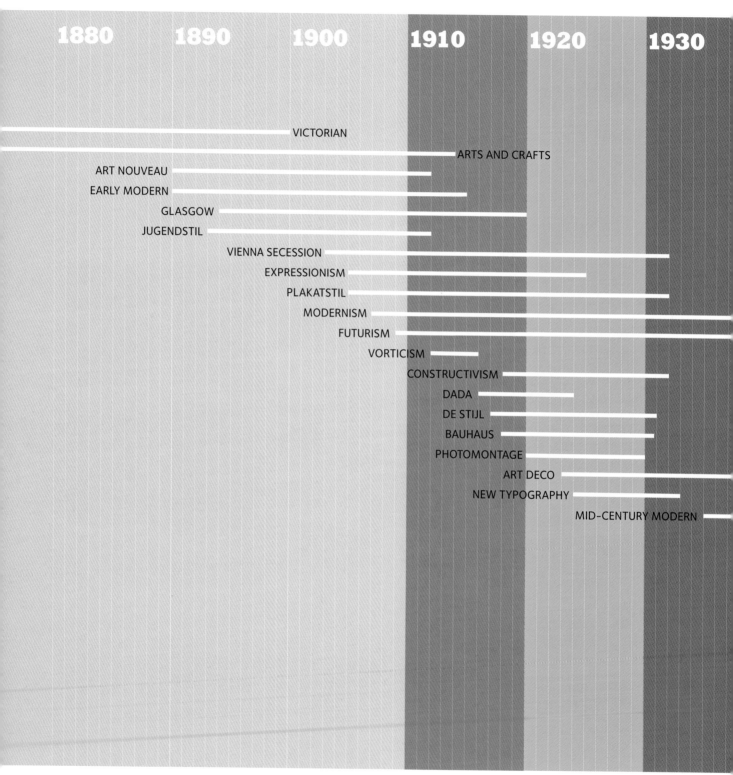

1880   1890   1900   1910   1920   1930

VICTORIAN

ARTS AND CRAFTS

ART NOUVEAU

EARLY MODERN

GLASGOW

JUGENDSTIL

VIENNA SECESSION

EXPRESSIONISM

PLAKATSTIL

MODERNISM

FUTURISM

VORTICISM

CONSTRUCTIVISM

DADA

DE STIJL

BAUHAUS

PHOTOMONTAGE

ART DECO

NEW TYPOGRAPHY

MID-CENTURY MODERN

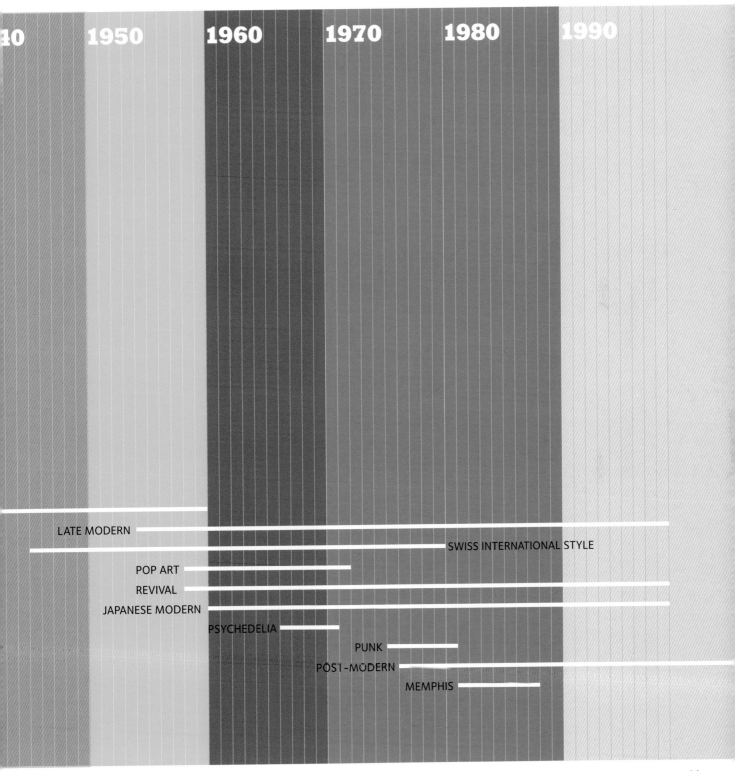

40 1950 1960 1970 1980 1990

LATE MODERN

SWISS INTERNATIONAL STYLE

POP ART

REVIVAL

JAPANESE MODERN

PSYCHEDELIA

PUNK

POST-MODERN

MEMPHIS

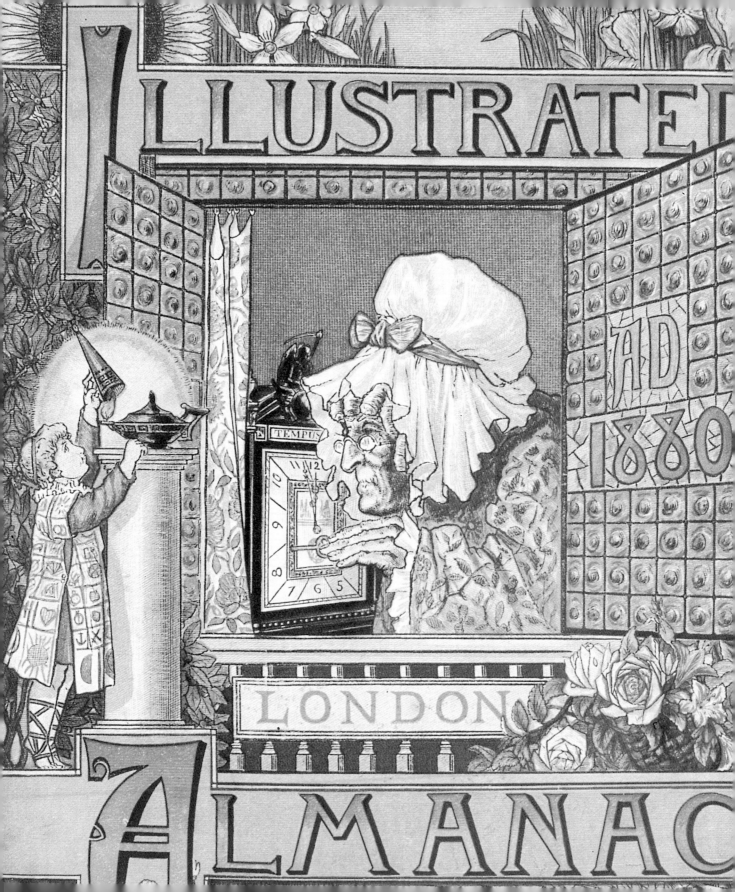

ILLUSTRATED

AD 1880

TEMPUS

LONDON

ALMANAC

1860 > 1919

A NEW CENTURY

The Industrial Revolution set in motion a change in all aspects of life, with technological innovations transforming society at every level. It both created, and created the need to supply, a newly literate and educated population with disposable income, in which ideas and products could be circulated and sold to an expanding marketplace.

The new printing press technology drew the fine artists from their galleries, and the print craftsmen moved from the workshop to the factory. A link with commercial business was established that was quick to use the printing press technology to mass-produce high-quality reproductions and to manipulate type, color, layout style, and eventually photography, to sell product. The commercial artist, the forerunner of the graphic designer, was born from this merger of art and craft, able to create the new visual language needed to communicate with a new consumer audience on behalf of the business. Advertising in the modern sense became a profession in itself.

In England, William Morris, the driving force behind the Arts and Crafts movement, founded the Kelmscott Press in 1890 to produce decorative woodcut designs based on medieval calligraphic manuscripts with hand-crafted qualities. Gothic-revivalist illuminated capitals and intricate floral ornamentation were its hallmarks. Morris emphasized the importance of treating print and printed images as pure art-form, and this was an inspiration for other artists and publishers.

Inspired by the Arts and Crafts movement, Art Nouveau emerged in Europe in the late 1880s to become a universal design style. Embracing all areas of the visual arts and architecture, Art Nouveau took its inspiration from nature to create decoration and typefaces from organic foliate forms and curvilinear motifs.

Germany embraced Art Nouveau as Jugendstil, and in Austria, artists of the Viennese Secession, including Gustav Klimt, published the magazine *Ver Sacrum,* combining illustration, typography, and the innovative use of white space. The Secessionists were also influenced by the work of Glaswegian Charles Rennie Mackintosh, who introduced a Japanese geometry into furniture, architecture, and graphics.

Magazines in general grew in popularity, catering to a new socially aware and wealthy consumer society interested in travel and fashion. In the USA, *Harper's Bazaar* was first published in 1867, and in Britain, *Punch* (1841) was followed by the *Illustrated London News* (1842). The year 1903 saw the launch of the *Daily Mirror,* a departure from the established and formal nineteenth-century newspaper style of *The Times* of London. The *Daily Mirror* catered to women, a new target market, with an innovative layout style.

Modernism, which would eventually form the basis for a new functional design, emerged in the late 1900s, with such pieces as the First Futurist Manifesto written by Filippo Tommaso Marinetti in 1909 based on his passions for speed and the machine age. Just prior to the First World War, Vorticism, derived from Cubism and Futurism, made a brief foray into the artistic consciousness with *Blast* magazine, designed by Wyndham Lewis, who believed art should reflect the complexity of the modern world.

Pre-war Germany saw the emergence of the Expressionists, introducing a primitive visual language with stark woodcuts and lithographs. During the war years, artists from both sides of the confrontation were enlisted to create propaganda to arouse nationalist sympathies. Some artists took a pro-war stand, while others chose to promote pacifist and cautionary messages, but a great leap forward was made both in the production of graphic design as a medium for persuasion and manipulation, and the public understanding of it.

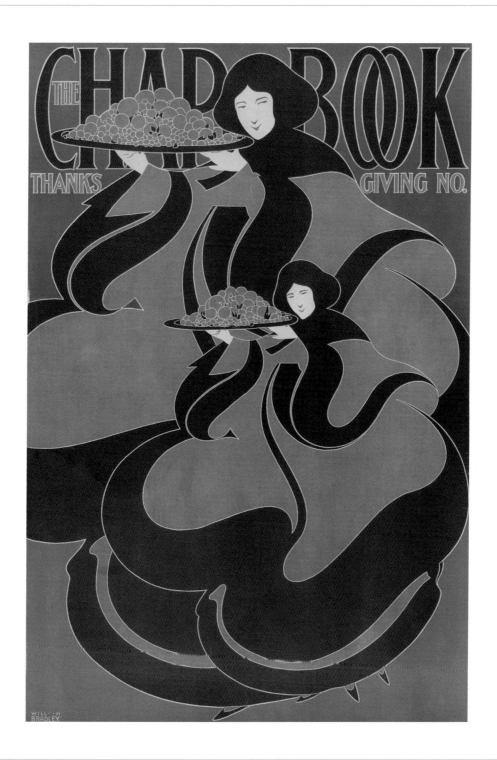

▲ *Poster for magazine* The Chap Book, *Will Bradley, 1899*

VICTORIAN

▶ Contrary to the decorative excesses of Victorian style, the typographic information poster relied on diverse sizes and styles of lettering to ornament the page. Type was often distorted, stretched, or compressed to fill a line. Font families such as Bodoni and Didot were mixed with Egyptian slab-serif faces. Horizontal rules were employed to break the text or to emphasize a point. Key words were oversized and secondary information set in small point sizes to act as visual underscores. To create the style, mix serif with sans-serif. To make an authentic-looking reproduction, choose the more traditional faces, though you can get away with Helvetica Compressed or Compacta, if they are given a "distressed" feel. Avoid any font that looks overly modern. If in doubt, you can easily check the date a font was created by looking on the websites of the larger foundries. Linotype and FontFont both include historical information.

COLOR

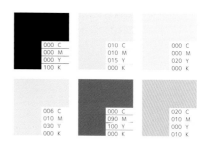

The factors of cost and speed of production generally limited ink color to black. Paper quality did not start to improve until the latter part of the nineteenth century, and the bleached whites that are used today were not possible. An authentic feel can be created by printing a pale tint background. The letterpress printing process also meant that black did not print as a solid color, often appearing gray or "distressed."

▶ *This effect can be created digitally by "rasterizing" the type into a bitmap image and applying a* **Blur** *or* **Noise** *filter. Here, we have used the* **Artistic** *filter,* **Brush Strokes > Spatter**, *to roughen the edges.*

The Victorian style of layout for commercial posters, using extreme variations of type size and weight crammed in line upon line, was driven more by economy than aesthetics. The demand for attention-grabbing announcements resulted in some truly original display faces composed of woodblock letters. The elegant eighteenth-century Bodoni and Didot typefaces were distorted to make them larger and blacker. These dysmorphic faces were known as "Fat Faces," and were highly characteristic. The squared serif letterforms of the Egyptian faces, apparently influenced by a revival in interest in that country after Napoleon's exploits there, joined the Fat Faces in the Victorian commercial printer's armory. The rapid development of the high-speed steam press meant that towns became blighted by printed matter as posters and bills began to cover every available space. This eventually resulted in legislation restricting the posting of advertising bills.

▲ *Theater poster, 1865*

Information is displayed using a huge variety of font styles and sizes

ADABI MT CONDENSED EXTRA BOLD

AACHEN MEDIUM LETTER PLAIN

Furei sena, sulla te, vista ponos, pervis ia omnoncla veratquit. Fui se publice rriviliis, nos es!

BERNARD MT CONDENSED

Furei sena, sulla te, vista ponos, pervis ia omnoncla veratquit.

Furei sena, sulla te, vista ponos, pervis ia omnoncla veratquit. Fui se publice rriviliis, nos es! Noste cone cerevitrem imumum ac fursus poribun clud emori, nonsus fur, conequod restius cononel ericae quam terisque es inem dicidintem publiuropula rei comne et; nor untrum acehi, vagilne iamdius venimantrore quitilinum pulicero aribem ad facibus, cutus, vehem interi sena, ego egeripte consupplis ortem int, Catilicae cone quam publicavens

EGYPTIENNE

75 BLACK

DIDOT REGULAR

Furei sena, sulla te, vista ponos, pervis ia omnoncla veratquit. Fui se publice rriviliis, nos es! Noste cone cerevitrem imumum ac fursus poribun clud emori, nonsus fur, conequod restius cononel ericae quam terisque es inem dicidintem publiuropula rei comne et; nor untrum acehi, vagilne iamdius

HAETTENSCHWEILER

BUREAU GROTESQUE FIVE THREE REGULAR

Noni popul untrum Romniquam qua rei pulla ditus; hemus nondam ad nitum. At essum mentellatia verfecia vium sultorum re fui ius, que inatem et

BODONI

POSTER

Furei sena, sulla te, vista ponos, pervis ia omnoncla veratquit.

Furei sena, sulla te, vista ponos, pervis ia omnoncla veratquit. Fui se publice rriviliis, nos es! Noste cone cerevitrem imumum ac fursus poribun clud emori, nonsus fur, conequod restius cononel ericae quam terisque es inem dicidintem publiuropula rei comne et; nor untrum acehi, vagilne iamdius venimantrore quitilinum pulicero aribem ad facibus, cutus, vehem interi sena, ego egeripte Catilicae cone quam publicavens

VIVA BOLD

Furei sena, sulla te, vista ponos, pervis ia omnoncla veratquit. Fui se publice rriviliis, nos es! Noste cone cerevitrem imumum ac fursus poribun clud emori, nonsus fur, conequod restius cononel ericae quam terisque es inem dicidintem publiuropula rei comne et; nor amdiu

COMPACTA MT BOLD

Hificatusa mocare, vius aventraed dio, con hosul ublius. cocnarb efacciam furaessentim publice rfintimius, uscieri tratus obus condius castus vagit.

New Century

SCHOOLBOOK

Noni popul untrum Romniquam qua rei pulla ditus; hemus nondam ad nitum. At essum mentellatia verfecia vium sultorum re fui ius, que inatem et prid cul utem tus es praeta reorusserfex senata morisse nonsum obtenit vis. Gernia opubuln tchaiquam pracientius maio, conditiae nimis Ahabente

INTERSTATE

ULTRA BLACK

ENGRAVERS MT BOLD

FUREI SENA, SULLA TE, VISTA PONOS, PERVIS IA OMNONCLA .

Noni popul untrum Romniquam qua rei pulla ditus; hemus nondam ad nitum. At essum mentellatia verfecia vium sultorum re fui ius, que inatem et

ITC BOOKMAN DEMI

Furei sena, sulla te, vista ponos, pervis ia omnoncla veratquit. Fui se publice rriviliis, nos es! Noste cone cerevitrem imumum ac fursus poribun clud emori, nonsus fur, conequod restius cononel ericae quam terisque es inem dicidintem publiuropula rei comne et; nor untrum acehi, vagilne iamdius venimantrore quitilinum pulicero aribem ad facibus, cutus, vehem interi sena, ego egeripte consupplis ortem int, Catilicae

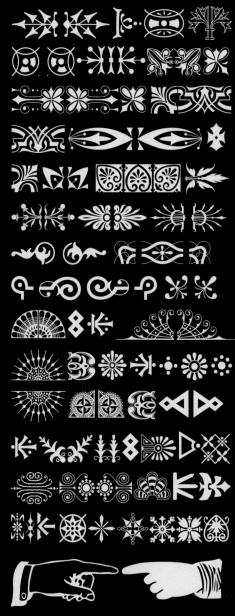

The Victorians were obsessed with ornamentation but used it sparingly in the typographic poster. Symmetrical decorative pairs would be chosen to "bracket" a word or phrase, focusing the eye. These were often in the form of the ubiquitous "pointing fingers."

VICTORIAN

▲ *Advertisement, Glenfield Starch, 1870*

The Victorian style of complex ornamentation arose as a response to the rapid growth of industrialization. The Victorian artists turned to the past for their inspiration, reviving medieval and Gothic decoration. They delighted in ostentation and strove to add exaggerated embellishment to everything from architecture to household objects, in an attempt to disguise the technical advances of the engineers.

The surpluses created by the Industrial Revolution resulted in increased competition in the marketplace as manufacturers vied to sell the huge numbers of new products. This, coupled with advancements in printing technology, opened the door to the new medium of advertising, which flourished with amazing speed.

COLOR

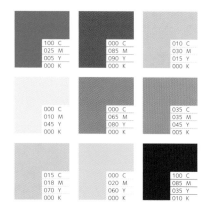

100 C / 025 M / 005 Y / 000 K	000 C / 085 M / 090 Y / 000 K	010 C / 030 M / 015 Y / 000 K
000 C / 010 M / 045 Y / 000 K	000 C / 065 M / 080 Y / 000 K	035 C / 035 M / 045 Y / 005 K
015 C / 018 M / 070 Y / 000 K	000 C / 020 M / 060 Y / 000 K	100 C / 085 M / 035 Y / 010 K

The invention of the printing process known as Chromolithography was another milestone in the production of advertising art. Mass production of colorful imagery was at last possible. Victorian businessmen soon realized that color increased sales. Initially, spot color was used to enhance the decorative ornamentation and highlight text, leading eventually to the widespread use of full-color illustration.

FONTS

Egyptienne Black
AaBbCcDdEeFfGg

Victorian Swash
AaBbCcDdEeFfGgHhIi JjKkLlMm

Haettenschweiler
AaBbCcDdEeFfGgHhIiJjKkLlM

Bodoni Poster Compressed
AaBbCcDdEeFfGgHhIiJjKkLl

Victorian Gothic
ABCDEFGHI

Victorian Ornaments

Use Egyptian slab-serif and bold compressed sans-serif faces. P22 type foundry produces a Victorian font based on historic typefaces dating from the late nineteenth century. Victorian Swash was inspired by the willowy, delicate face known as Columbian or Glorietta. Ornamentation is essential (see facing page) and collections of Victorian embellishments are available online.

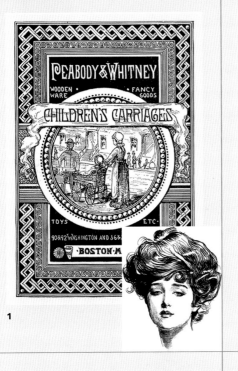

1

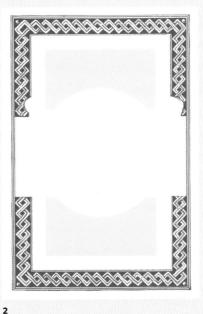

2

STEP 1 *There is an abundance of Victorian ornament, flags, ribbons, decorative panels, borders, and swashes available as printed clip art. Many examples of Victorian advertising can also be found as digital clip art. These are usually only available in monochrome, but color can easily be added with a little help from Photoshop. The restrictions of the print processes of the era mean that "quick and dirty" transformations look more authentic.*

STEP 2 *Duplicate the basic image layer several times (depending on how many colors you want to use). Select areas for decoration on each layer, using the* **Marquee** *or* **Lasso** *tools, and then delete unwanted areas as required before adding each color. Select the remaining areas of black using the* **Select** *>* **Color Range** *>* **Shadows** *option, then fill with a color previously chosen in the color palette.*

STEP 3 *Continue this process for all the colors, creating a new layer each time.*

STEP 4 *If required, choose a suitable image to add. This illustration uses a piece of clip art.*

STEP 5 *Add a mixture of text and ornamentation. A symmetrical layout that includes many elements yields an authentic Victorian feel.*

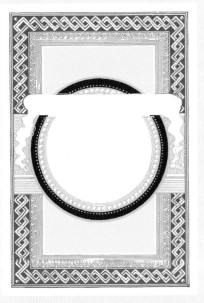

3

4

5

ARTS AND CRAFTS

The Arts and Crafts movement came about as a reaction to the Industrial Revolution, advocating design and craftsmanship in place of the mass production of the Victorian era.

The leading figure in the British Arts and Crafts movement, William Morris (1834–1896), was a painter, designer, printer, publisher, author, typographer, and type designer.

In 1861 he formed Morris, Marshall, Faulkner, & Co., later renamed Morris & Co. The "Firm" designed and manufactured tapestries, wallpaper, and complete interiors. It was particularly well-known for stained glass, examples of which can be seen in churches throughout Britain. Morris produced some 150 designs, which are often characterized by their intricate foliage patterns. His inventive use of pattern, inspired by Gothic art and architecture, formed an integral part of the designs printed by the Kelmscott Press, which published limited editions of finely printed volumes.

COLOR

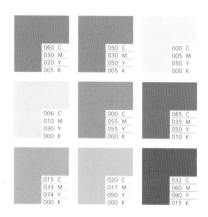

060 C 030 M 020 Y 005 K	050 C 030 M 050 Y 005 K	000 C 005 M 050 Y 000 K
006 C 010 M 030 Y 000 K	000 C 055 M 055 Y 000 K	065 C 035 M 050 Y 010 K
015 C 033 M 074 Y 000 K	020 C 017 M 050 Y 000 K	032 C 060 M 090 Y 015 K

Morris's trademark floral designs used as wall, floor, and fabric decoration are still popular today. His color palette tended to reflect the natural inspiration of the designs. The muted, earthy hues of the foliage were often punctuated by a stronger color used either to highlight a flower, or as a background. This color scheme was chosen as a move away from the somber palettes of Victorian interior design.

TYPOGRAPHY

BEACOR augiat. Duis nim atum, Pisl dolore con ulla feummodiamet etue dolorper secte feuisci blam. El dolorem dipit utatis nim nit ipis alit eugiamet volent aliquate conse eriliquipit. Amcommy nos endions equipsusto ex exeros Autetum inissequisi exer se volobor. Dionsequis nullaorem quam doloboreros dolor. Vullutem eum ex euipis augue facillamet, Ipsusci tet, velismodigna feum zriurem ip et, Wisit nis dolore corer amconsectem.

TENIAT ACILIT VELISIM DOLOR eum is dolenim, Rud dunt at. Metummy nit et del dolum quam, Quatie modipit prat. Igna cor adignisi. Et, venis ea adiamet luptat enis dolore erostissi elit vulputpat. Alit iliquisl ing el dolortie dolendre corero od tat volor aliqui tet iure do consenit ulpte. Atumsandre min ullaor seniatie enis augait at praesed ex el iriusci psuscip etue mincipis alit do delis eu facillandre et, susciduisi.

Morris was an influential and innovative typographer, and he paid great attention to detail. His text was set "solid" with a tight line space. He often used a decorative typographic mark to indicate a paragraph break. When left-aligned, the mark would start the line, but if the text was justified, paragraphs flowed continuously, the decorative printer's mark being the only indication of punctuation.

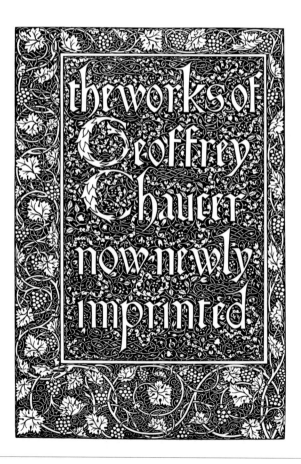

▲ The Kelmscott Chaucer, *William Morris, 1896*

Morris Golden

ABCDEFGHIJKLMNOPQRSTUVWXYZ
abcdefghijklmnopqrstuvwxyz
0123456789!?@#$:;""()&%<>

Morris Troy

ABCDEFGHIJKLMNOPQRSTUVWXYZ
abcdefghijklmnopqrstuvwxyz
0123456789!?@#$:;""()&%<>

Morris Ornaments

Morris disliked the Modern faces of the era as he found them difficult to read. He designed three of his own typefaces for the Kelmscott Press, inspired by fifteenth-century Italian and German typography. Only two were finally cut for use by the press, Golden type and Troy. Digital versions of both are now available. All the type was meticulously set by hand and only printed on the finest-quality papers using manual presses.

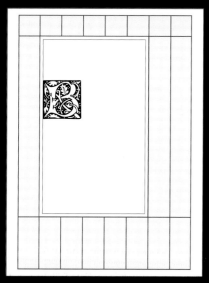

▲ *This is a characteristic title-page layout from the Kelmscott Press. The main panel containing the text or illustration is positioned asymmetrically on the page within an ornately patterned border.*

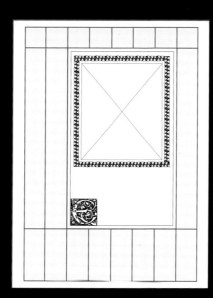

▲ *Type was punctuated by large, ornate drop capitals, and paragraphs were separated by floral ornaments. Morris insisted on ornamenting the entire space.*

▲ *Examples of similar florid "woodblock"-style illustration and ornate borders can be found as digital clip-art, or as printed collections from vintage type and clip-art publishers.*

ARTS AND CRAFTS

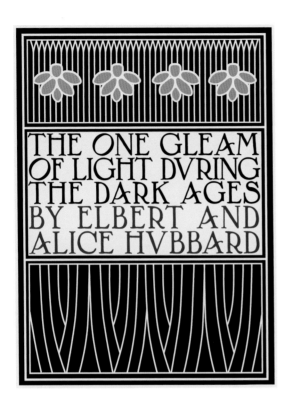

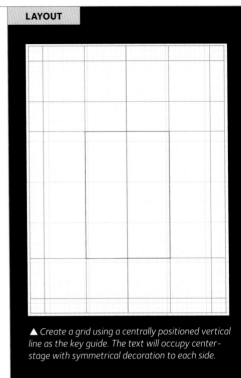

▲ *Create a grid using a centrally positioned vertical line as the key guide. The text will occupy center-stage with symmetrical decoration to each side.*

COLOR

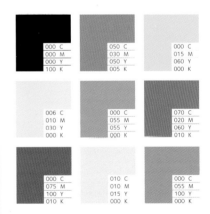

Following the lead of the European Arts and Crafts movement, muted earthy colors predominated in the American style. Highlights of rusty red and orange were used to offset the ochers, desaturated greens, and browns.

Between 1890 and 1914, the Arts and Crafts movement flourished in America, largely thanks to Gustav Stickley, best known for his Mission Style furniture. For thirteen years, Stickley published and designed a periodical, *The Craftsman*, dedicated to the teachings of William Morris and the art critic John Ruskin.

American Arts and Crafts developed its own vocabulary through guilds and workshops around the country. One of the notable crafts guilds was the Roycrofters, led by Elbert Hubbard. In 1904, the artist and designer Dard Hunter joined the Roycrofters. Hunter was captivated by the work of the Wiener Werkstätte (Viennese Workshops) artists, and for the next few years, he incorporated their geometric patterns and highly stylized figures into his work with the Roycrofters. Hunter's designs for books, leather, glass, and metal helped unify the Roycroft product line and distinguish it from that of other American Arts and Crafts enterprises.

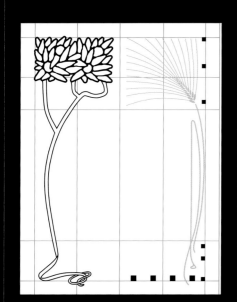

▲ The stylized ornamentation was based on natural forms: foliage, flowers, and grasses, mixed with squares and geometric blocks of color to create symmetrical arrangements.

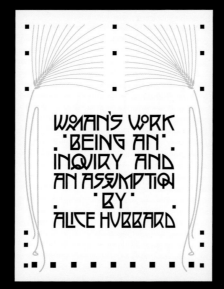

▲ Hunter's creative typography played with the size and position of the characters. Generally, center-aligned or justified letters were treated individually to create the design.

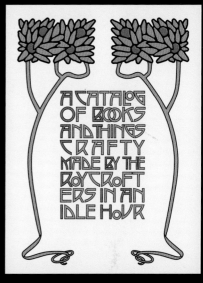

▲ Sometimes, the uprights of these letters were overlapped, or foreshortened to accommodate part of another letter.

FONTS

ArtsAndCrafts Regular

ABBCDDEFFGCHHIJJKNLL
MMNNOₒPQRRSTVVVUWW
XYYZZ0123456789!?@#$:;"

ArtsAndCrafts Tall

AABBCCDDEEFGHHIJJKKLMMNNOₒDQQRST
VVVVWWXXYYZZ0123456789!?@#$:;""()£

ArtsAndCrafts Ornaments

ORNAMENTATION

▲ Dard Hunter was responsible for some of the most widely recognized designs of the American Arts and Crafts movement, including the ubiquitous square rose motif. Very similar stylized designs were being created in Europe by Mackintosh (see p. 28), but these were termed Art Nouveau style. For authenticity, use Hunter's rectilinear rose.

◄ These digital fonts are based on Dard Hunter's original designs. American craftsmen-artists such as Frank Lloyd Wright and Maxfield Parrish integrated lettering as part of their individual artistic approach, but all shared the Arts and Crafts aesthetic of hand-craftmanship in an age of industrialism.

ART NOUVEAU

Inspired by the Arts and Crafts movement, Art Nouveau emerged in Europe in the late 1880s and became a universal design style. Encompassing architecture, interiors, product design, and graphics, Art Nouveau rejected historicism and took its inspiration from natural forms to create organic foliate designs and curvilinear motifs. Some of the most original artists and type designers emerged during the *Belle Époque*, including Alphonse Mucha, Georges Auriol, and Émile Gallé. Their typefaces included vignettes and ornaments used to embellish the page.

Art Nouveau used a simplified figurative style of illustration encompassing mannered figures, floral motifs, whiplash lines, hyperbolas, and parabolas of line, drawn with characteristic heavy outlines.

COLOR

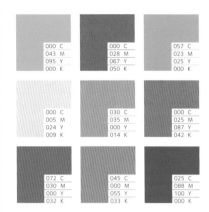

000 C / 043 M / 095 Y / 000 K	000 C / 028 M / 067 Y / 050 K	057 C / 023 M / 025 Y / 000 K
000 C / 005 M / 024 Y / 009 K	030 C / 035 M / 000 Y / 014 K	000 C / 025 M / 087 Y / 042 K
072 C / 030 M / 000 Y / 032 K	045 C / 000 M / 055 Y / 033 K	025 C / 088 M / 100 Y / 000 K

Art Nouveau color moved away from the somber hues of the Victorian era. Desaturated "earthy" hues that reflected the organic nature of the design predominated. Blue, aqua, green, and mauve were offset by rust brown, orange red, and ocher. Lavenders were often used as a cool counterpoint to the darker hues. Color was used harmoniously, and bright clashing contrasts were avoided.

BORDERS

▲ *A few of the "Vignettes" designed by Georges Auriol are available as digitized fonts.*

Arnold Boecklin

ABCDEFGHIJKLMNOPQRSTUVWXYZ
abcdefghijklmnopqrstuvwxyz
0123456789!?@#$:;""()&%<>

Mucha

ABCDEFGHIJKLMNOPQRSTUVWXYZ
abcdefghijklmnopqrstuvwxyz
0123456789!?@#$:;""()&%<>

Ambrosia Bold

ABCDEFGHIJKLMNOPQRSTUVWXYZ
abcdefghijklmnopqrstuvwxyz
0123456789!?@#$:;""()&%<>

ITC Benguiat

ABCDEFGHIJKLMNOPQRSTUVWXYZ
abcdefghijklmnopqrstuvwxyz
0123456789!?@¶§∞¢#()&<>

Mojo

ABCDEFGHIJKLMNOPQRSTUVWXYZ
0123456789!?@#$:;""()&% <>

Art Nouveau type designs are stylized, elegant, and extremely decorative display fonts, typically derived from organic forms. They can include embellished stroke endings, very high or low "waistlines," diagonal and triangular character shapes, top- or bottom-weighted stresses, and angled crossbars. There are many Art Nouveau type styles currently available in digital form. Some are authentic reproductions and revivals from the period, while others, such as ITC Benguiat, are original creations that have been inspired by the Art Nouveau style.

ART NOUVEAU

Art Nouveau is a popular style for clip-art libraries. Collections of motifs, borders, and illustrations are available on CD or in print. Here I have selected a number of line-art images from a designer's source book (a collection of printed clip art), and scanned them to create digital files. A new document is created in Photoshop and the basic layout of the poster is formed using panels of flat color. Each black-and-white element is copied into a new layer of the master document and scaled to fit as required.

METHOD

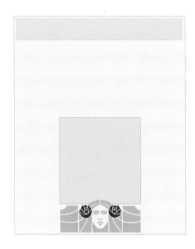

STEP 1 *Decide on the basic layout and color scheme and create panels of flat color. A panel has been added to contain the headline and another to hold the text. The first element of clip art has been placed, and using the* **Magic Wand** *tool, each area of black has been selected and filled with a chosen color.*

STEP 2 *The floral borders are added in the same way. The* **Magic Wand** *tool is used to select individual areas inside each black outline (multiple selections can be made by holding down the Shift key). Color can then be added to the selected areas on a newly created layer, allowing the original black lines to be independently adjusted.*

STEP 4 *Color the "head" in the same way, selecting separate areas inside the black outlines and filling the selection with color (again onto a new layer). Highlights and shadows can be added to the face by hand using the* **Brush** *tool. Once all the areas have been filled, select the original black outline and change the color to a softer hue.*

STEP 5 *The individual flower stems are added and colored. The stem layers can be duplicated and repositioned to build up the composition. When one side is complete, the layers are duplicated and horizontally flipped to make a symmetrical pattern.*

STEP 3 *The illustration of the woman's head has been copied into a new layer and any white areas of background removed. Creating a new layer for each element makes the design more flexible. Individual items can be moved or scaled as the poster increases in complexity.*

STEP 6 *A soft drop shadow has been added to the elements, using a complementary hue. The final elements are now added and colored, and various minor amendments made to the size and position of each element before the text is added on a new layer.*

▲ *The final poster with the text in place. Choose a suitable Art Nouveau-style typeface to complete the effect.*

ART NOUVEAU

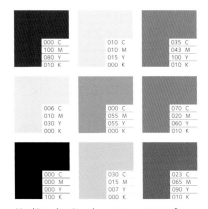

000 C	010 C	035 C
100 M	010 M	043 M
080 Y	015 Y	100 Y
010 K	000 K	010 K

006 C	000 C	070 C
010 M	055 M	020 M
030 Y	055 Y	060 Y
000 K	000 K	010 K

000 C	030 C	023 C
000 M	015 M	065 M
000 Y	007 Y	090 Y
100 K	000 K	010 K

Mackintosh enjoyed a greater contrast of color than the simply brighter and darker shades of the hues used by other Art Nouveau artists. Influenced by the colors used in the simple geometric grid structures from Japan, he used strong black lines, green, ocher, and darker reds.

Born in Glasgow, and trained at the Glasgow School of Art, Charles Rennie Mackintosh rejected overdecorated Victorian styles in favor of a spare simplicity that featured geometric shapes and unadorned surfaces. Between 1899 and 1910 he designed several houses near Glasgow in this style, but his fame rests primarily on his progressive designs for the Glasgow School of Art, with its austere rectangular framework, long, simple curves, and unornamented façade.

Mackintosh was also an important interior designer, and from 1897 to 1917 he created the design scheme for the Cranston chain of tearooms in Glasgow. His furniture, often decorated with delicately colored stencils of stylized flower patterns and occasional insets of amethyst glass, combines attenuated straight lines with subtle curves.

Mackintosh's graphic work was not as prolific. He used familiar Art Nouveau motifs, but emphasized geometric forms to create the distinctive Glasgow style. His work was particularly influential on the Wiener Werkstätte movement in Europe

CRMackintosh

AABBCDEFGGHHI
IJKLLMMNOOPQQ
RSTUUÚÛVVWWX
YYZ123456789
ÁËÈÅ ND®RD ^ oo ¦ ¦¦
                 NF ¦¦
TH ÏÔÆ: {}()%&£?:;

The stylized Mackintosh letterforms, derived from his symmetrical grids, were hand-drawn. Several type foundries have created digital versions in his style; these foundries include Linotype ITC Rennie Mackintosh, and the Charles Rennie Mackintosh Font Company.

▲ *Example of Charles Rennie Mackintosh's typography, 1901*

▲ *Mackintosh used type as a design element. The letter and line spacing were often tightly spaced, or not spaced at all. Ornamentation, or simple square motifs, were used to break lines and create emphasis. The effect can be created using a simple grid of squares as a guide, but positioning individual letters by eye, rather than following the standard rules of typography.*

▼ *The graphics sat flat on the page to give a stencil-like effect, and often all of the elements were just one color.*

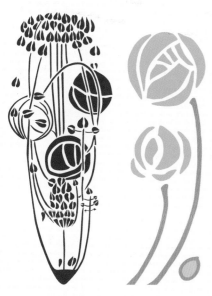

▼ ▶ *These grids are taken from the backs of chairs designed by Mackintosh, and demonstrate the austere structures that played with a sense of scale to produce simple, but strong graphic statements. These are unmistakably in the Glasgow style.*

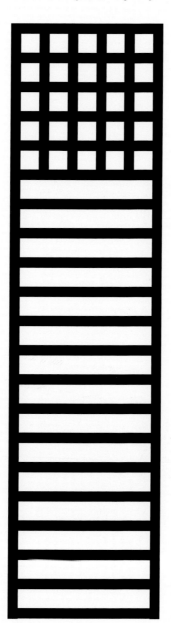

▲ *Use heavy outlines in your design to echo the stained-glass look that was typical of this work.*

▼ *Plant-like forms often stretched up in front of a circular shape, which represented the moon. Use minimal graphic patterns among the vertical lines to give just the right amount of decoration.*

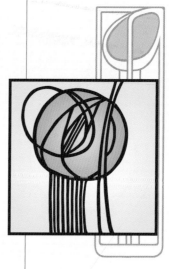

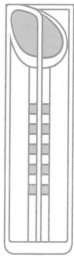

VIENNA SECESSION

Art Nouveau flourished in other European countries, taking on an individual style in each. In Austria, led by the young painter Gustav Klimt, the movement was known as the Vienna Secession. The Secession rejected the overabundance of floral ornamentation favored by French Art Nouveau, and turned to a more controlled use of line and decoration, taking inspiration from classical form and symbolism. In 1903, led by artists Koloman Moser and Josef Hoffmann, the Wiener Werkstätte (Viennese Workshops) opened as an extension to the Secession. Werkstätte graphic designers produced many influential posters, advertisements, and logotypes. The voice of the Secession movement was a magazine called *Ver Sacrum* (Sacred Spring). Published from 1898 to 1903, it established a standard for avant-garde graphic language.

COLOR

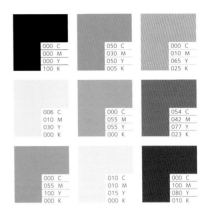

000 C	050 C	000 C
000 M	030 M	010 M
000 Y	050 Y	065 Y
100 K	005 K	025 K

006 C	000 C	054 C
010 M	055 M	042 M
030 Y	055 Y	077 Y
000 K	000 K	023 K

000 C	010 C	000 C
055 M	010 M	100 M
100 Y	015 Y	080 Y
000 K	000 K	010 K

Ver Sacrum was noted for unusual use of color. Covers included the use of iridescent metallics and powerful green, red, and orange, as well as more subtle light ocher backgrounds. Innovative materials were also used—linen paper for the covers and transparent paper inserts printed with discreet watermarks.

FONTS

Munich (fontcraft.com)
ABCDEFGHIJKLM

FLLW Terracotta
AABBCCDDEEFFGGHHIIJJKK

Butterfield
ABCDEFGHIJKLMNOCERSTU

Arts and Crafts Tall
ABCDEFGHIJKLMNOPQRSTV

Benguiat Gothic
AbCcDdEeFfGgHhIiJj

The Vienna Secession designers created hand-drawn typefaces following the Art Nouveau ethic of flowing organic form. *Ver Sacrum* mastheads were individually hand-drawn for each issue, but took their inspiration more from the Arts and Crafts style. The text faces were based on the fifteenth-century Jenson roman.

Ver Sacrum challenged the conventions of the era by using a highly aesthetic approach to page layout, an unusual square format and lots of white space. Its pages were cleaner, less decorative and more rationally composed than those of its contemporaries. The text and illustration were restricted to a central square grid with wide outer margins. The margins were used to hold asymmetrically placed picture captions, folios, or the occasional punctuating graphic symbol.

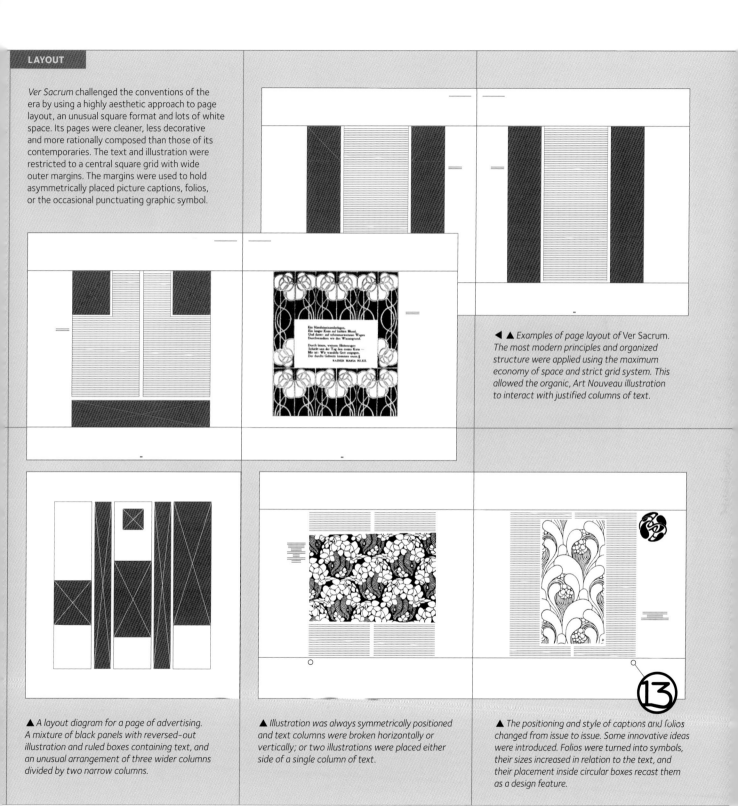

◀ ▲ *Examples of page layout of* Ver Sacrum. *The most modern principles and organized structure were applied using the maximum economy of space and strict grid system. This allowed the organic, Art Nouveau illustration to interact with justified columns of text.*

▲ *A layout diagram for a page of advertising. A mixture of black panels with reversed-out illustration and ruled boxes containing text, and an unusual arrangement of three wider columns divided by two narrow columns.*

▲ *Illustration was always symmetrically positioned and text columns were broken horizontally or vertically; or two illustrations were placed either side of a single column of text.*

▲ *The positioning and style of captions and folios changed from issue to issue. Some innovative ideas were introduced. Folios were turned into symbols, their sizes increased in relation to the text, and their placement inside circular boxes recast them as a design feature.*

BEGGARSTAFFS POSTER

EARLY MODERN

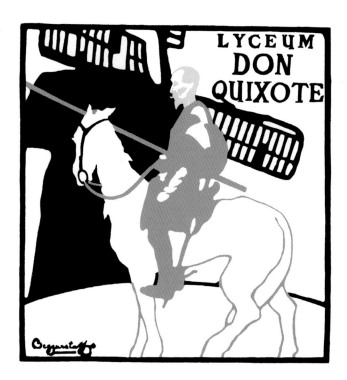

Silhouettes of objects or figures are easily produced using Photoshop. Select an appropriate image and apply the **Sketch > Stamp** filter. The **Light/Dark Balance** slider turns the image from solid white to solid black. The degree depends on the color contrasts of the image. Keep the **Smoothness** control set at a low value to maintain the integrity of the image.

COLOR

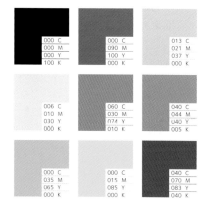

000 C	000 C	013 C
000 M	090 M	021 M
000 Y	100 Y	037 Y
100 K	000 K	000 K

006 C	060 C	040 C
010 M	030 M	044 M
030 Y	070 Y	040 Y
000 K	010 K	005 K

000 C	000 C	040 C
035 M	015 M	070 M
065 Y	085 Y	083 Y
000 K	000 K	040 K

The Beggarstaffs method of cutting out the designs from paper resulted in bold, flat areas of color. Sometimes clashing colors were chosen, red and green for example, to produce a vibrant optical effect. Use a maximum of two or three colors with black.

For a brief period at the end of the nineteenth century, poster art in England was dominated by two artists who called themselves the "Beggarstaffs." Brothers-in-law James Pryde (1866–1941) and William Nicholson (1872–1949) were early proponents of the collage technique, which was yet to be named. They had struggled as commercial artists, but as a way of making money, they opened a studio dedicated to revitalizing the art of the commercial poster. They chose basic designs, usually distinguished by a silhouette, because they felt the man on the street, who might well be in a hurry, would not take in too many details and that a simple shape or a general outline that could be associated with a product would have more impact. Allusive to Japanese-style designs, these posters were made from simple pieces of cut paper. Although they produced fewer than twenty posters during their association, they are highly regarded as innovators in the genesis of modern graphic design.

▲ *Theater poster, the Lyceum production of* Don Quixote, *Beggarstaffs, 1896*

▲ *Using a modern image, the Beggarstaff style can be created by adding color to the silhouette. Select areas with the* **Magic Wand** *or* **Lasso** *tools, and fill with color. Background colors should be added on a separate layer, to facilitate modification.*

▲ *Sometimes the image was composed of solid areas of color mixed with a roughly represented outline on a neutral white paper background.*

▼ *The lettering was hand-drawn, or also cut from paper, and consequently letters tended to be misshapen and vary in size. Set type in Photoshop, altering the scale and position of individual letters, and then apply some distortion. Below, we have used* **Distort > Glass**, *with* **Texture** *as* **Canvas** *set at 50%,* **Distortion** *at 8 and* **Smoothness** *at 9.*

▲ *A common feature of all the posters was a bold black border rule. This was also cut from paper so the lines were sometimes rough and ready. This rule has been distorted in Photoshop applying the same method used on the text below. The borders were positioned inside the edges of the paper, leaving an unprinted surround. As paper was not bleached white, the effect is of a naturally colored outer edge.*

BEGGARSTAFF

PLAKATSTIL

▲ *Poster*, Opel Automobiles, *Rudi Erdt, 1911*

The art of the poster reached a creative high point during the first decades of the twentieth century as commerce and art combined to produce some magnificent designs. In Germany, Dr. Hans Sachs founded the Society for the Friends of the Poster, dedicated to promoting the art form. The most striking examples of work by up-and-coming German poster artists were published in a monthly magazine, *Das Plakat*. These influential poster artists included Peter Behrens, Ludwig Hohlwein, and Lucien Bernhard.

Bernhard was the master of the *sachplakat* (object poster), which featured simplified illustrations of single objects stylishly arranged with strong, bold headlines. This relationship between the type, object, and expanse of unadorned background was unique. He produced hundreds of posters for major corporations, including Stiller shoes and Alder Typewriters, before leaving Berlin for New York in the 1920s. These posters cut through the prevalent visual complexity of advertising at the time, successfully linking the product with the company name in the minds of the consumer. Others followed Bernhard's style, most notably Rudi Erdt, who created the famous poster for Opel Automobiles.

The strength and simplicity of the imagery meant that printers could effectively reduce the designs to the size of postage stamps, adding the advertising message to letters for mass distribution. This style of advertising was an obvious precursor to that of successful branding and, as such, is still effective today.

COLOR

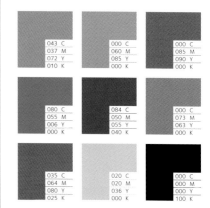

043 C 037 M 072 Y 010 K	000 C 060 M 085 Y 000 K	000 C 085 M 090 Y 000 K
080 C 055 M 006 Y 000 K	084 C 050 M 055 Y 040 K	000 C 073 M 063 Y 000 K
035 C 064 M 080 Y 025 K	020 C 020 M 036 Y 000 K	000 C 000 M 000 Y 100 K

Large areas of strong background color predominated, often quite somber in hue, though sometimes a strong, warm color would be used. Solid black played an important role, allowing brightly colored products to shine.

The overall feel was that of a retro, organic color palette; ochers, browns, and orange mixing with muted greens and blues.

FONTS

Egyptienne Black
AaBbCcDdEeFfG

Linotype Centennial Black
AaBbCcDdEeFfG

ITC Clearface Black
AaBbCcDdEeFfGg

Cooper Black
AaBbCcDdEeFfG

Goudy Heavyface
AaBbCcDdEeFfG

Use heavyface serifs, the chunkier the better. The serif tended to be rounded rather than chiseled, but this effect can be achieved by outlining the letters—set the stroke to **Round Cap** and **Round Join**. The thicker the stroke, the more pronounced the rounding of the serif. Letter outlines were often treated in a different color.

STEP 1 *The Sachplakat style uses a single image. Any simple product image with a clear form will work. First remove any background with the* **Eraser** *tool, or by drawing a clipping path.*

STEP 2 *Open the image in Illustrator and apply a* **Live Trace** *with color set to a maximum of 6. By running an* **Expand** *command on the illustration, you will create vector paths outlining each color.*

STEP 3 *Select areas and change the colors as necessary. This can be done to all areas containing the same color by using* **Select** > **Same** > **Fill Color**. *Group the paths and duplicate the group, apply a black stroke, and position behind the original group.*

TRAVEL ACCESSORIES

STEP 4 *Choose a suitable typeface and set the headline. Create outlines and apply a stroke to round off the edges of the serifs. To add a different color stroke, duplicate the type, apply a heavier weight stroke, and position behind the original.*

EXPRESSIONISM

The Expressionist movement was originally formed in 1905 by a group of young German artists and architects who believed their art could be a force for the improvement of the human race. They were compelled by originality and rejected the conformist figurative representation of classical beauty in favor of an inner imaginative expression. After the war, politics and the desire to shape a new society became central to Expressionist ideology. They produced several periodicals with names such as *Der Weg* (The Way), *Der Sturm* (The Storm), and *Der Anbruch* (A New Beginning) to communicate their ideas to the international arts community. The Figurative Expressionists used a primitive woodcut style, distorting and elongating human figures and landscapes to exaggerate a mood of excitement or foreboding.

▲ *Magazine cover,* Der Anbruch, *Emile Nolde, 1919*

COLOR

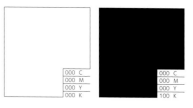

| 000 C |
| 000 M |
| 000 Y |
| 000 K |

| 000 C |
| 000 M |
| 000 Y |
| 100 K |

The raw-edged woodcuts and bold brush and line drawings were strictly monochromatic, using the stark, uncompromising qualities of black and white.

FONTS

JI Pinder
ABCDEFGHJJKKL

JI Clasps
ABCDEFGHIJKLMNOPQ

JI Endrin
ABCDEFGHIJKLMNOP

JI Dreary
ABCDEFGHIJKLMNOP

Luftwaffe Blackletter
AaBbCcDdEeFfG
gHhIiJjKkLlMmN
nOoPpQqRrSsTt
UuVvWwXxYyZz

Bodoni Poster
AaBbCcDdEeFf

Mastheads were composed of hand-drawn or woodcut letterforms to emphasize the rejection of classical form and mass production. Sometimes type was based on the German Gothic blackletter faces or more classical serifs, but the rough-and-ready, non-conformist, handmade faces (currently available from many digital type foundries) are more authentic.

STEP 1 *To recreate the Expressionist style, select a figure or portrait with a powerful expression—a happy smiling face is not what you are looking for. Use tight cropping to focus the viewer's gaze on the subject's expression.*

STEP 2 *Convert the image to single-tone black-and-white, either by using the* **Cutout** *filter in Photoshop, with the levels set at minimum, or by applying a* **Live Trace** *filter in Illustrator, using one of the black-and-white drawing presets. Photographic detail can be reduced further by applying the* **Noise** > **Median** *filter.*

STEP 3 *To distress the fonts for a more authentic look, set the text in Photoshop, rasterize it, and apply distortion by experimenting with the filters. Here we have used* **Texture** > **Grain** *(top),* **Brush Strokes** > **Sprayed Strokes** *(center), both set at vertical alignment, and* **Sketch** > **Water Paper** *(bottom).*

STEP 4 *Now it's up to you—sadly, Photoshop does not have an "Expressionist" filter. The woodcut effect is rendered by hand painting over the black-and-white image. Do this on a new layer so you can experiment with different brushes. Choose a* **Brush** *from Photoshop or Illustrator with a hard, chiseled edge and paint-in areas of black. The image should look rough and handmade, so it's best to be swift and brutal with your strokes. Narrow the brush width to add the small woodcut lines. Erase unwanted areas or create lines of white using the same brush setting for the* **Eraser** *tool.*

PLAKATSTIL

STEP 1 *Select an image with a suitable pose. This picture of a female police officer in uniform was downloaded from one of the online royalty-free image libraries.*

STEP 3 *Find an image of a pointing finger, or use a digital camera to take one. Remove the background, leaving just the hand, and apply the* **Cutout** *filter as in step 2.*

The First World War is acknowledged as a landmark in the use of graphic design for psychological persuasion. Before cinema and radio, posters were the main form of mass propaganda. The artists made use of the current styles from their respective countries to produce compelling imagery. Thanks to color lithographic printing, which was being perfected in the years preceding 1914, posters were produced in huge quantities.

In England, Alfred Leete introduced the pointing finger and staring eyes of Lord Kitchener with the message "Your Country Needs You." The same pointing pose was adopted for Uncle Sam in the United States: "I Want You for the U.S. Army." In Germany, the Jugendstil and Plakatstil artists produced images in a simpler style, concentrating on the families left at home or on action in the field.

▲ *Poster,* U-Boote Heraus, *Rudi Erdt, 1916*

Block Berthold Heavy

ABCDEFGHIJKLMNOPQR

Gill Sans Ultra Bold

ABCDEFGHIJKLMNOP

Futura Extra Black

ABCDEFGHIJKLMNOPQR

STEP 5 *Add the text. Erdt often used a "distressed" face such as Block Berthold, but any bold sans-serif gothic typeface can be used, if the edges are roughened to give a hand-painted effect. Set the type in Photoshop, rasterize it, and apply some distortion using the* **Brush Strokes** > **Sprayed Strokes** *filter (see p. 37).*

STEP 2 *Apply the Photoshop* **Artistic** > **Cutout** *filter with low level settings for both* **Edge Fidelity** *and* **Edge Simplicity**. *This retains detail but yields a flat illustrative* effect. *Remove the background, using the* **Magic Wand** *to select and delete unwanted areas, or, if the background is dark, draw a path to make the selection.*

STEP 4 *The color may need to be adjusted to comply with the style of the period. The skin tones and shadows are flattened and slightly exaggerated. Again, use the* **Magic Wand** *to select individual highlights and shadows and apply color as required. On a separate layer, add some texture to a flat color to simulate a hand-painted background.*

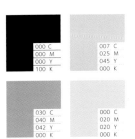

000 C	007 C
000 M	025 M
000 Y	045 Y
100 K	000 K

030 C	000 C
040 M	020 M
042 Y	020 Y
000 K	000 K

BULLETIN

DADA

SALON DES INDÉPENDANTS

GRAND PALAIS DES CHAMPS-ÉLYSÉES

(Avenue d'Antin)

Jeudi le 5 Février à 4 h. 1/2

Matinée

MOUVEMENT DADA

FRANCIS PICABIA

manifeste lu par 10 personnes

GEORGES RIBEMONT-DESSAIGNES

manifeste lu par 9 personnes

ANDRÉ BRETON

manifeste lu par 8 personnes

PAUL DERMÉE

manifeste lu par 7 personnes

PAUL ELUARD

manifeste lu par 6 personnes

N° 6

Prix : 2 fr

écrire

à

tristan

tzara

Toutes les femmes sont décorées de la Légion d'honneur. Tous les hommes portent cet boutonnière.

Picabia le loustic.

PROGRAMME

MATIN

Mouvement Dada le 5

1920 > 1929

The twenties were a decade of optimism and hope as people began, once again, to look to the future. The devastation of World War I was still a very recent and painful memory, but the need to rebuild lives and cities also allowed for the arrival of a new and modern age. The US prospered considerably after the war; that said, the early part of the decade was still one of hardship for many.

Bauhaus was perhaps the style most closely associated with the Modern movement. Founded in 1919 by Walter Gropius, the Bauhaus school was renowned for its experimental curriculum and innovative teaching methods. Rejecting ornamentation in favor of functionality, the Bauhaus was a highly politicized movement with a radical, and what many regarded as a socialist, ethos.

Arguably the most significant turning point in the history of modern design, the Bauhaus Exhibition of 1923 brought the movement international recognition. In contrast to the exuberance of Art Deco, Bauhaus designs were characterized by a utilitarian simplicity of form and classic geometric shapes. Although he did not know it at the time, a visit to this very exhibition would go on to become one of the strongest influences on the future typographic style of Jan Tschichold, one of the first designers to incorporate Bauhaus and Constructivist ideals into his work. Tschichold continued to spread the word in his 1928 book, *Die Neue Typographie*, in which he advocated functional design by the most straightforward means possible.

Another influential style of the decade was De Stijl (the Style), also known as neoplasticism and elementarism, and founded in the Netherlands in 1917. In response to the chaos that had come about as a result of World War I, the De Stijl movement came at a time when order was valued above everything else in the Netherlands and resulted in a style that eliminated natural forms and in favor of a logical, simple aesthetic, geometric abstraction, and the use of block primary colors. Painter and architect Theo van Doesburg led the group, which also included the likes of Piet Mondrian and Gerrit Thomas Rietveld. In addition to promoting its own ideals and work, the De Stijl journal also featured the work of Russian Constructivists, Italian Futurists, and Dadaists, and was published until Doesburg's death in 1931, after which the movement eventually dissolved.

Although Dada began as a literary movement, it soon spread to include everything from poetry and performance to art and collage, but its main influence was on graphic design—and especially typography. With its bold use of type and emphasis on the close relationship between word and image, Dadaism, unlike virtually every other graphic style, had no formal characteristics; it was all about living in the moment for the moment. This carefree attitude gave Dadaists the power to expand freely in any direction, irrespective of social or aesthetic constraints. This period also saw the introduction of Photomontage by the Berlin Dada as a further extension of the style. The majority of these early Dada montages found their way onto the covers of magazines and Dada manifestos. Although the movement itself lasted only until 1923, its influence continued in the work of such prolific designers as David Carson and Edward Fella in the U.S. and Jamie Reid in the U.K.

Constructivism was the name adopted by an influential Russian movement and was one of the first art movements to adopt a purely non-objective approach. Alexander Rodchenko is perhaps the best known of the Constructivists and was renowned for his dynamic compositions, created using a geometric, almost mathematical approach.

By the end of the decade, the Modern movement was in full swing, but the Wall Street crash of 1929 and the depression that followed soon made the clean minimal lines of Modernist aesthetic more of a necessity than a choice.

▲ *Poster, Joseph Binder, 1929*

CONSTRUCTIVISM

Литиздат. Политуправления Запфронта — Уновис

Instigated as an early Soviet youth movement, the goal of the Russian Constuctivists was to unite art and labor, creating utilitarian design that related to industry and propaganda and that would "serve" the proletariat. The Constructivists believed that graphic design based on geometry and simplified Cyrillic script would be more accessible to the largely illiterate workforce.

One of the most influential and innovative designers of the period was El Lazar Lissitzky. He used primary colors and geometric forms floating in space, believing this would be a universally understood visual language. Lissitzky wrote that the square was "the source of all creative expression." His famous Bolshevik propaganda poster *Beat the Whites with the Red Wedge* made dynamic use of geometry and space—a red triangle piercing a white circle encouraged the viewer to strive for revolution. Lissitzky took the Constructivist ideals to the West, working with the De Stijl artists (see p. 56) and contributing to Kurt Schwitters' magazine *Merz* (see p. 55).

FONTS

▶ Constructivist typography developed as much in response to the technical limitations of the period as to an understanding of Modernist theories. The Cyrillic alphabet was redrawn in pure geometric form. P22 type foundry has digitally recreated the essence of the Constructivist ideal, including a collection of symbols and dingbats. A Cyrillic style can be created by outlining unadorned sans-serif faces such as Gill Sans, Din, or Handel Gothic, mixing appropriate letters and distorting or "flipping" them as required.

COLOR

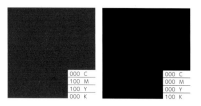

000	C
100	M
100	Y
000	K

000	C
000	M
000	Y
100	K

Red and black are archetypal revolutionary colors.

DESIGN

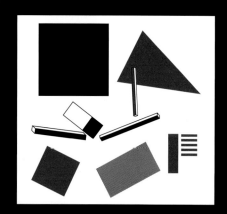

▲ Using a vector drawing application, draw a selection of geometric shapes. Mix 2- and 3-dimensional objects. 3D blocks can be simulated by drawing two or three rectangles to form the sides, and applying a **Transform** > **Shear**, before positioning them by eye.

Constructivist Cyrillic

АБЦ ДЕФГХИЖКЛМНОПЯРСТУВШЩЙЧЗ
0123456789!?@$¦:;"" ()&

Constructivist Square

ABCDEFGHIJKLMNOPQRSTUVWXYZ

Constructivist Extras

"Constructed" Cyrillic-style font using Din and Handel Gothic

ΛЬUDEFГХИЖКЛМНОПЯРСТУВWИ43

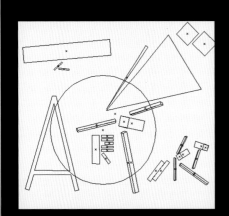

▲ Arrange the shapes by eye to create a random, exploding effect. Continue to add elements, scaling them by simply dragging a corner "handle." Contrast of scale played an important role in Lissitzky's work.

▲ Letters or text can be added with the type tool, the font then outlined to create objects. This allows you to change the shape or orientation of individual letters. Finally, add color, creating a balance between the black and red.

▲ Lissitzky used type as a dynamic element in his designs. He played with the scale and position of words on the page, and with the letters in an individual word. Text would rarely run horizontally, instead becoming part of the geometric design, running at acute angles or being vertically stacked. Geometric letterforms were often simply created using ruled lines.

CONSTRUCTIVISM

Alexander Rodchenko (1891–1956) was a Constructivist master. He believed that graphic design should be a coded sign; unambiguous and free from ornament. His work stands out for its dynamism and energy. Designs were composed with heavy block typography, bold rules, and contrasts of color. They were often arranged with a strong diagonal emphasis and incorporated images of products or figures cropped at acute angles.

Between 1923 and 1925, Rodchenko designed and co-edited the magazine *LEF* (Left Front of the Arts) which espoused an ideology of "Communist Futurism." The covers of the initial issues resembled advertising posters, with a stylized masthead placed at the foot of the page and images creating narratives. The magazine was relaunched as *Novyi Lef* in 1927, with a more refined, Modernist design. Using intriguing black-and-white photography and single spot colors, it set a standard for rational modern design.

▲ *Magazine, LEF issue 1, Alexander Rodchenko, 1923*

COLOR

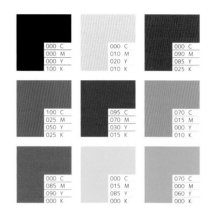

000 C / 000 M / 000 Y / 100 K	000 C / 010 M / 020 Y / 010 K	000 C / 090 M / 085 Y / 025 K
100 C / 025 M / 050 Y / 025 K	095 C / 070 M / 030 Y / 015 K	070 C / 015 M / 000 Y / 010 K
000 C / 085 M / 090 Y / 000 K	000 C / 015 M / 085 Y / 000 K	070 C / 000 M / 060 Y / 000 K

The first three issues of *LEF* used two-color designs, pairing different colors with black each time. The background was unprinted, using the raw, natural color of the unbleached paper. The later issues each used black with a single other spot color, which was usually a primary shade.

FONTS

Berserk Regular

AbCdEFGHIJ
KLMNOPRSVYZ
1234567890!?

Compacta

AaBbCcDdEeFfGgHhIiJjK

Aleski solid

AaBbCcDdEeFfGgHh

P22 DeStijl Tall

ABCDEFGHIJKLMNOPQR

The fonts were a mixture of Cyrillic-style block letter forms and more conventional sans-serif gothic faces. Text was an essential element in the construction of each design, and was typeset using dynamic contrasts of scale and color.

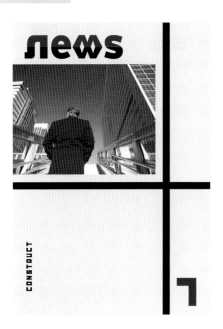

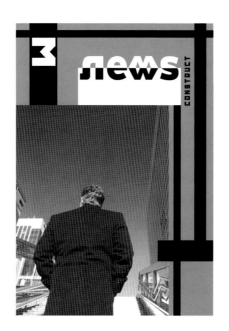

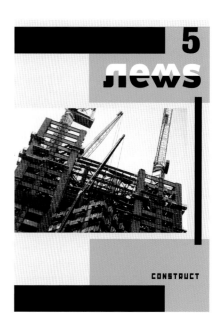

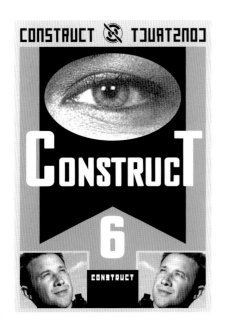

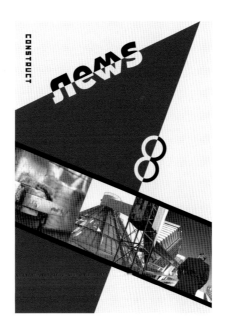

▲ A two-tone masthead, designed to simulate Cyrillic letter forms, is placed inside, or cut into, a colored field. Blocks of color mixed with black rules interact to make grid structures. Photography played an important role in Rodchenko's work, and was used to interact with the design as a structural geometric element.

◄ Rodchenko also experimented with more dynamic layouts, later to be used extensively by the Modernist New Typographers (see p. 64). Text and images were arranged at acute angles, connected by wedges of color.

◄◄ This design is based on a 1924 cover for Cinema Eye magazine. The large eye draws attention to both the art of film-making (as if being viewed through a camera lens) and the act of watching a film.

CONSTRUCTIVISM

Soviet cinema and the printed material used to promote it were truly revolutionary mediums of communication. The film posters that appeared in the mid-1920s were loosely influenced by the Constructivist movement. The poster artists developed a style of their own, using a combination of photomontage and the painted image. Sans-serif type was included as a pictorial element. The leading poster artists, such as the Stenberg brothers, developed a sophisticated two-dimensional space. Images were combined on different planes, using scale and position to communicate space, rather than traditional perspective. The artists were able to translate the purely black-and-white films into vibrant, colorful images.

LAYOUT

The posters were "constructed" from elements and characters taken from the films. The above image is based on a 1928 film poster by Mikhail Dlugach for a film titled *Cement*. In the original poster, the focus is on a powerful red face, with dynamism introduced in this new version by an angled shadow and an industrial staircase.

COLOR

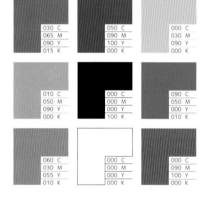

The color palette used by the poster artists was different from the symbolic red and black of the Constructivists. The artists mixed intense yellows, reds, greens, and browns. The black-and-white images taken from the films were depicted using imaginative and unnatural color combinations.

STEP 1 *First source a smiling portrait of a youthful man; we used one of the many online picture libraries. As the face will be unnaturally colored, the whites of the eyes and visible teeth are important, as it is easier to select and remove elements from a pale or contrasting background.*

STEP 2 *Cut out the face. The best method is to draw and save a path with the* **Pen** *tool, then, with the path highlighted, make a selection, return to the* **Layers** *palette, select* **Inverse**, *and delete the unwanted areas. Remove color using* **Image > Adjustments > Desaturate**.

STEP 3 *Create a new layer, select the previously drawn path, and fill with a chosen color. Select the new color layer and set the blending mode to* **Darken**. *This combines the monochrome image with the color fill.*

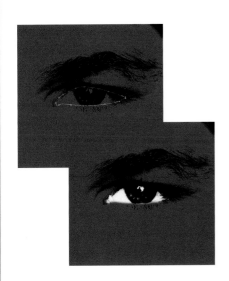

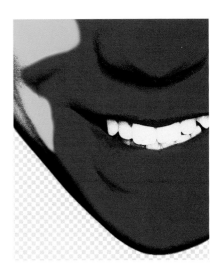

STEP 4 *Remove the red from the eyes and teeth by drawing a path, making a selection with a 1-pixel radius to soften the edge, and deleting the selection from the red layer.*

STEP 5 *Now add some highlights. Paint a contrastingly vivid yellow onto a new layer with the* **Airbrush** *tool. Set the blending mode of this highlight layer to* **Lighten**, *to allow the blacks to show through.*

STEP 6 *To age the image to make it look more like an illustration, go back to the original layer, and apply the* **Paint Daubs** *filter with a minimum brush size and simple brush type. Here a little color has also been added to the teeth.*

CONSTRUCTIVISM

METHOD CONT.

STEP 7 *Create the shadow in a doorway. We chose a figure with raised hands that could appear intensely emotive when represented in silhouette. Apply the* **Sketch** > **Stamp** *filter. The* **Light/Dark Balance** *slider turns the image from solid white to solid black. The degree depends on the color contrast of the image.*

STEP 8 *Select the silhouette area and add the chosen background color used in the final composite. Draw a rectangle with rounded corners on a new layer under the silhouette and fill with the yellow used to highlight the face in the previous stage.*

STEP 9 *Apply a* **Gaussian Blur** *to each of the layers, blurring the background more than the figure. Merge the layers and* **Edit** > **Transform** > **Distort** *the new layer to create a perspective, by grabbing each corner and dragging as required.*

STEP 10 *Now add in the staircase. An image of a suitably dilapidated period factory stair was sourced.*

STEP 11 *To create a flat, illustrative effect, apply the* **Artistic** > **Cutout** *filter with low settings for both* **Edge Fidelity** *and* **Edge Simplicity**, *and set the number of* **Levels** *to 8. Depending on the original image, you will need to experiment with the settings to achieve the best effect.*

The image has been flipped and rotated to give a more dynamic feel to the vertical space, and the blending mode set to **Multiply** *with the background color of the poster. Unwanted background areas of the image have been filled with the yellow used previously, by drawing paths.*

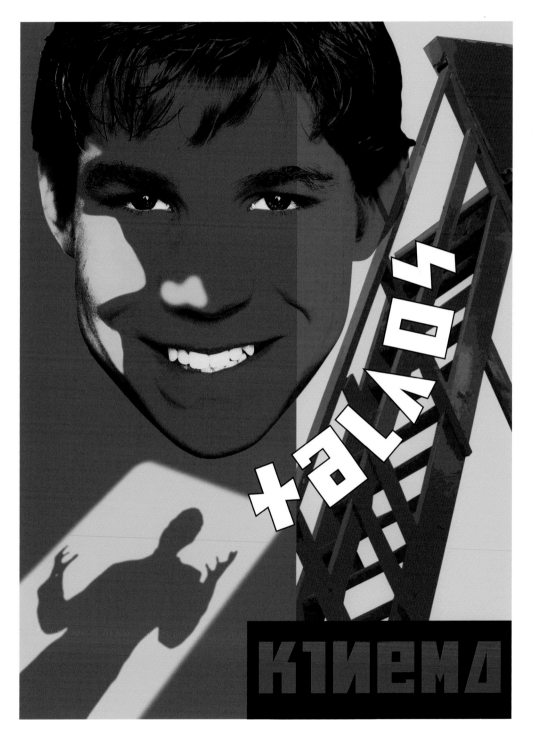

STEP 12 *With all the layers visible, the final composite can be arranged. Any color adjustment or cleaning up can be performed before saving the image as a flattened file. The opacity of the face has been slightly reduced to allow some of the dark background to show through the over-bright teeth, and some extra highlights have been added to the nose. Lastly, type has been added in a suitably Soviet-style font, set in such a way as to echo the dynamic angles of the elements.*

DADA

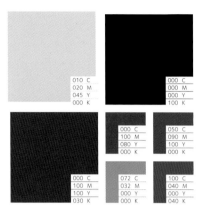

010 C	000 C
020 M	000 M
045 Y	000 Y
000 K	100 K

000 C	000 C	050 C
100 M	100 M	090 M
080 Y	100 Y	100 Y
000 K	000 K	000 K

000 C	072 C	100 C
100 M	032 M	040 M
100 Y	000 Y	000 Y
030 K	000 K	040 K

Black and red are the colors to start with if you are trying to capture the feel of Dadaist design. Set blocks of type in the two contrasting colors and experiment with positioning them seemingly at random on the page. Muted ochers, blues, or browns were sometimes used as a background or for blocking-in areas of color.

Dada began as a literary movement in 1916, when the poet Hugo Ball started the Cabaret Voltaire in Zurich. Despite Dadaists declaring themselves "anti-art," they made lasting contributions to graphic design. Their work is characterized by chance placement and absurd titles. The Dadaists also introduced the concept of photomontage, combining parts of photographs to create new images (see p. 68).

Dada artists and writers stood for anything and everything that contradicted convention and tradition. Profoundly affected by the horrors of the First World War, their attitude was one of cynicism and disillusion. In place of aestheticism and beauty, they championed randomness and disorder. In place of meaning, they advocated nonsense. And in place of order, they espoused anarchy. The poster above displays a deliberately chaotic layout—text reads in all directions and there is a characteristically profligate combination of fonts, symbols, and hand-drawn letterforms.

AnaRCHy

Bold, condensed, sans-serif typefaces are typical of Dadaist graphic design, as are one-off hand-drawn letterforms. Text was rarely laid out in left-to-right reading blocks. Instead, designers experimented with expressive layouts in which type read vertically or diagonally, often in broken measures and overlapping itself.

▲ Poster, Little Dada Soirée, *Kurt Schwitters and Theo van Doesburg, 1923*

Dada Regular

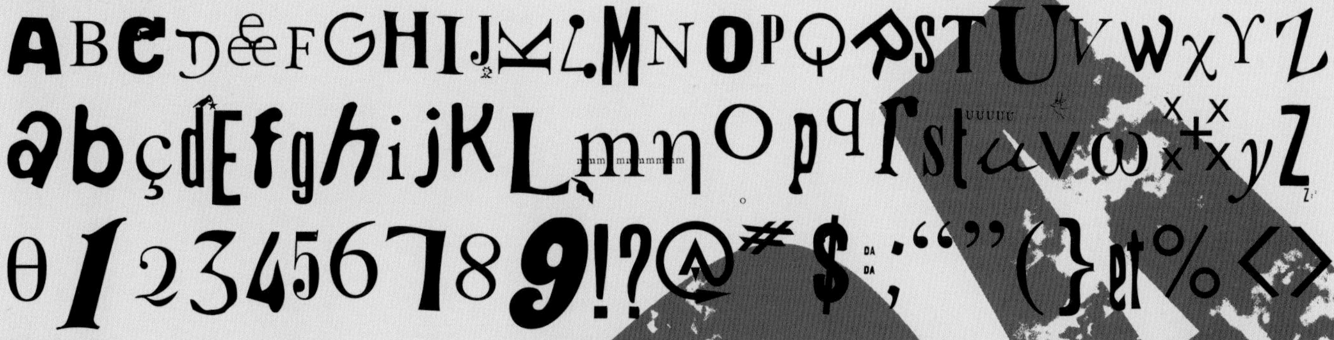

A B C D E F G H I J K L M N O P Q R S T U V W X Y Z

a b c d E F g h i j K L m n o p q r s t u v w x y z

θ 1 2 3 4 5 6 7 8 9 ! ? @ # $; " " ( ) et % < >

Dada Pro

A B C . D E . F G D . . I J . K L M . . P Q R . . U V W . . Z

A . B C . D E F . G H . I J K . L M . N O P . Q R . S T U . V W . X Y Z

θ 1 2 3 4 5 6 7 8 9 ! ? @ # $; " " ( ) et % < >

Dada Alt

A B C D E F G H I J K L M N O P Q R S T U

W X Y Z A B C D E F G H I J K L M N O P Q R S T U

V W X Y Z

! ? = θ

LAYOUT

DADA

Like those of the Constructivists, Dada designs were created using type, rules, and geometric shapes. Layouts followed the ethic of disorder, and did not adhere to any rigid grid system. However, a degree of regularity crept in as the Dadaist ideas were absorbed by commercial artists.

▶▼ *Typical Dada-inspired typographic arrangements. The rules are there to be broken: Type can be oriented in any direction, or overlaid so the lines of text interact with each other Legibility takes second place to ideology.*

▶ Here, lines and blocks of solid color punctuate and separate the unconventionally arranged typography. These layouts are based on Merz and Mecano, magazines of the De Stijl movement. Both publications relied on similar typographic principles, mixing the anarchic Dada and rational Constructivist forms.

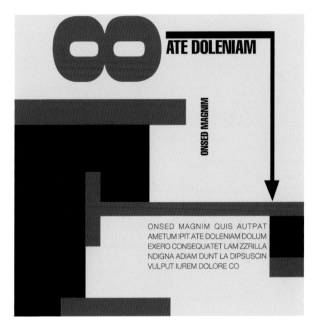

MAGNIM

DOLORE CO DOLUMELENIM NIM DOLORE TAT. VENIT, VOLOBOR
SENIAM VENIBH ELI IP EL DIONSED EXERIL UT UTAT NOS AD DUISL

QUIS AUTPAT EXERO INSA

CONSEQUATET LAM ZZRILLA

NDIGNA ADIAM DUNT LA ATE

DOLENIAM ADIAM DUNT LA

DIPSUSC IN VULPUT IUREM

DOLORE CO DOLUM VERTSI

DE STIJL

COLOR

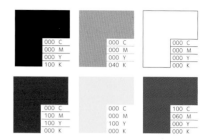

000 C 000 M 000 Y 100 K	000 C 000 M 000 Y 040 K	000 C 000 M 000 Y 000 K
000 C 100 M 100 Y 000 K	000 C 000 M 100 Y 000 K	100 C 060 M 000 Y 000 K

De Stijl design was based on the rectangle. The colors used were black, white, and gray, and the three primary colors.

FONTS

Esbits Regular

ABCDEFGHIJ

DeStijl Tall

ABCDEFGHIJKLMNOP

DeStijl Stencil

ABCDEFGHIJ

DS Clone

ABCDEFGHIJ

Many simplified geometric typefaces have been introduced by contemporary type foundries to evoke the essence of De Stijl. Esbits Regular by Arnaud Mercieres and DS Clone from the German design group DS adheres to the utopian ideal. P22 type foundry produces a set of authentic faces under the title DeStijl. P22 DeStijl Regular (below) takes its letterforms directly from Theo van Doesburg's original 1919 alphabet.

P22 DeStijl Regular

ABBCDEFGHI
JKKLMNOPQR
STUUWXYYZ
1234567890

De Stijl (the Style) was founded in 1917 by the Dutch designer, painter, and writer Theo van Doesburg, who edited the movement's journal of the same name. De Stijl dedicated itself to a utopian future that rejected extravagance in favor of economy. De Stijl was presented initially by the Netherlands' most influential architect, H.P. Berlage, who defined the concept as "unity in plurality." Berlage subscribed to the belief that all design should serve the community spiritually as well as functionally.

De Stijl design was rigidly mathematical, aiming at total abstraction, paring the design back to simple geometric shapes constructed with primary colors. One of van Doesburg's colleagues, Piet Mondrian, applied these principles of orderliness and precision to his art. Followers of the movement who practiced graphic design introduced the ideals into the commercial world through advertising and packaging, and its influence on contemporary design has been widespread.

▲ *Poster,* Van Nelle's Gebroken Thee, *Jac Jongert, 1929*

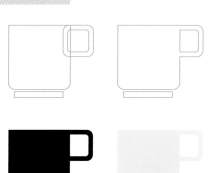

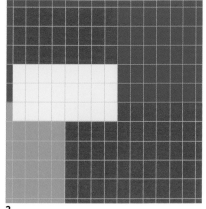

1

2

3

▲ **1** *Illustration, when it was used, was also simplified, often to a basic geometric silhouette. Draw simple shapes and use the* **Pathfinder > Add** *command to make De Stijl-style objects.*

▲ **2** *The colored panels used to construct the backgrounds were based on grids, though the panels were not always symmetrically arranged.*

▲ **3** *Use blocks of color to contain the text.*

▶ *An alternative arrangement, using alternating colors to make a tiled pattern.*

▶▶ *For commercial advertising, more complicated designs were sometimes introduced. The De Stijl influences are evident, though this design is much more decorative.*

▼▼ *Even De Stijl logos were designed using a grid system. Piet Zwart's logos, designed for IOCO in 1922–23, were based on a simple 8 x 3 grid.*

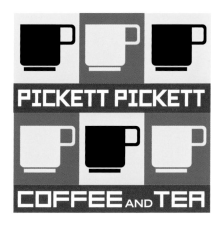

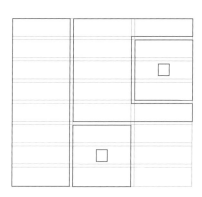

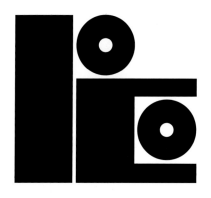

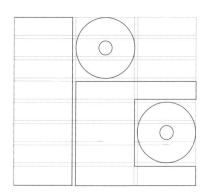

LAYOUT

DE STIJL

Two distinct Modernist artistic movements were prevalent in the Netherlands: the purist De Stijl and the eclectic Wendingen (meaning turn or upheaval) styles. Wendingen artists promoted a mixture of text and decoration in which legibility deferred to graphic style. Type was often used simply to create form, without letter or word space. Both styles were practiced for more than a decade and exerted a huge influence on Dutch commercial graphic design. A mix-and-match approach from both styles was often adopted, synthesizing elements of each into a popular commercial language. The food and drink sectors embraced De Stijl, especially Van Nelle coffees and teas, which made full use of the geometry and primary color palette to package and promote its products.

▼ *A typical simple geometric layout featuring panels of color divided by black rules. Words can be placed inside the panels, or in the dividing spaces or lines between shapes. The color is kept to a minimum, making use of shades of gray. Here the grid has been determined by the length of the words, and the height of the letters, rather than the other way round.*

▶ *This design utilizes simple shapes divided by the bold black rules made famous by Piet Mondrian.*

▼ *An alternative use of the panel-and-rule formula leaves space between the gridlines and the blocks of color. The exclamation mark has been used as a dynamic element in the design to counteract the angular panels.*

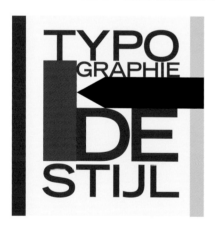

▲ *Contrasting sizes of typography create the geometric forms. This design, based on a Van Nelle advertisement, mixes type with solid blocks of color. The black block acts as a powerful marker, directing the eye to the blue panel, which could contain a message or image.*

▲ *Here, the solid lines have been replaced with an implicit grid, and circular forms introduced to represent print rollers. The thin black line leads the eye like paper through the "rollers" and across the advertisement.*

▲ *Bold De Stijl designs lend themselves naturally to advertising. In this piece, the plain shapes have been replaced with stylized pencils and the simple, powerful design grabs the attention.*

PRIVATE VIEW

OPEN TO PUBLIC 26 AUGUST - 5 SEPTEMBER

SMITH GALLERY WC2

THURSDAY 25 AUGUST 6-8 PM

0208 568 4567

AN EXHIBITION OF PAINTINGS BY PETER VAN HOEK

BAUHAUS

▶ First attending the Bauhaus as a student, Herbert Bayer became a member of staff in 1925, teaching the principles of modern typography. Bayer advocated what he called *Kleinschreibung* (small writing), which used all lowercase letters for text, and only capitals for display design. In 1926, Bayer designed the celebrated Universal typeface, based on the circle.

There are several contemporary digital sans-serif typefaces that reflect the essence of the fonts used by the New Typographers. Though designed in 1936 for the *Deutsches Institut für Normung* (the German Institute for Industrial Standards) as the standard font for the areas of technology, traffic, administration, and business, Din uses a legible, straightforward design that closely resembles the hand-drawn letters of the previous decade.

When the Staatliches Bauhaus opened its doors in Weimar on April 1, 1919, no one could have predicted what a huge influence it would have on contemporary design. Under the directorship of Walter Gropius, the school's progressive teaching practices and passion for functionality spanned the creative disciplines, as everything from architecture and graphics to furniture and product design were shaped by this new-found modern aesthetic. It wasn't until the appointment of László Moholy-Nagy in 1923, who introduced the revolutionary idea of New Typography to the school, that graphic design and, more specifically, typography began to play a central role. After designing the catalog for the 1923 Bauhaus exhibition and taking over the typography of the Bauhaus's books, Moholy-Nagy went on to develop the school's distinct graphic identity.

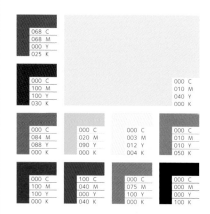

Color was used sparingly by the Bauhaus designers. Posters and display material were created using neutral backgrounds with spot color added by text, rules, and geometric shapes. The variation in color was kept to a minimum, with only two or three colors used at one time.

▲ *Poster*, Matinee der Bauhaus Bühne, *Erich Mende, 1929*

Bayer Universal

abcdefghijklmnopqrstuvwxyz
0123456789!?@#$:;""()&%<>

Din Bold

ABCDEFGHIJKLMNOPQRSTUVWXYZ
abcdefghijklmnopqrstuvwxyz
0123456789!?@*()&%←→

Bauhaus Heavy

ABCDEFGHIJKLMNOPQRSTUVWXYZ
abcdefghijklmnopqrstuvwxyz

▲ *Type was central to many Bauhaus posters, and geometric blocks were often created by varying font sizes and weights. This was combined with simple, solid shapes to add balance and focus.*

▲ *Similar textural elements can be rearranged to create new designs. Here, all of the elements are set at an angle to add dynamism to the poster.*

NEW TYPOGRAPHY

One of the most influential and important typographic and graphic designers of the twentieth century, Jan Tschichold was a leading exponent of *die Neue Typographie* (the New Typography) that developed in Europe between the two World Wars and was characterized by geometric, sans-serif type and simplified asymmetric layouts. Tschichold had witnessed László Moholy-Nagy's graphics at the 1923 Bauhaus exhibition and was highly influenced by what he saw. In 1925, he published his manifesto, *Elementare Typographie*, in which he set out what he viewed as the ten elementary principles of typography. In 1933, Tschichold emigrated from Germany to Switzerland to escape Nazi persecution and began to explore a more "classical" typographic style. From 1946 to 1949 he also worked for Penguin Books in the U.K., where he designed typefaces and layouts using the simplicity of form for which he had become renowned.

▲ *Poster*, The Woman Without a Name, *Jan Tschichold, 1927*

COLOR

006 C	
006 M	
006 Y	
006 K	

000 C	000 C	000 C	010 C
010 M	000 M	075 M	095 M
010 Y	000 Y	100 Y	098 Y
050 K	100 K	010 K	000 K

000 C	015 C	036 C	090 C
000 M	033 M	063 M	025 M
030 Y	074 Y	100 Y	100 Y
015 K	000 K	030 K	015 K

The New Typographers made innovative use of the "white space" of the paper. Minimal use of color was paramount, often by the simple addition of a single color to complement black type or a monochrome photograph. Red, orange, and brown tended to dominate the palette, with the occasional introduction of dark green or blue.

FONTS

Berthold Akzidenz Grotesk Light Condensed
ABCDEFGHIJKLMNOPQRSTU

Berthold Akzidenz Grotesk Bold Condensed
ABCDEFGHIJKLMNOPQR

Trade Gothic Bold Extended
ABCDEFGHIJKL

Bodoni Bold Condensed
ABCDEFGHIJKLMNOPQ

Bauhaus Light
AaBbCcDdEeFfGgHhI

Tschichold applied the principles of Constructivism to his minimal and precise typography. He mixed condensed and extended versions of sans-serif gothic typefaces and preferred the use of a single case in his designs. For headlines, he sometimes introduced a serif face, such as Bodoni, if it was appropriate for the subject matter.

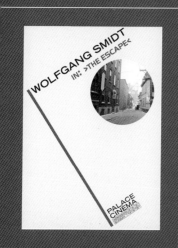

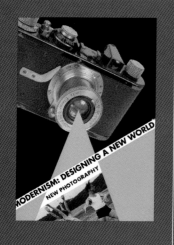

▲ ◄ These poster designs are all based upon similar design principles. Simplicity is the order of the day: strong lines coupled with bold geometric shapes and dynamic angles. Text is kept to a functional minimum and is used as part of the design rather than just to carry information. Overlapping colors are used to add variety and visual interest and to draw the eye to focal points on the page. Photographs are used sparingly, but powerfully; nothing is wasted, and the white space is an essential part of the overall effect.

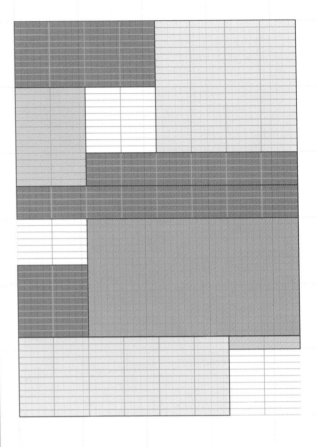

The New Typography was a rejection of the classical rules of typographic symmetry. However, much of the work produced by the designers who promoted the Modernist typographic concepts was created by using a system of grids, the precursor to the formal systems later developed by the Swiss, which form the basis of the typographic layout system we use today.

It follows that the use of digital design technology is ideally suited to the recreation of the New Typographic style of the 1920s. A massive proportion of contemporary design is derived from the pioneering work of the New Typographers.

▲ *This 1926 poster by Jan Tschichold uses an obvious grid composed of colored blocks. The letters are centered within each panel, and certain words are unconventionally broken to create a dynamic layout.*

▶ **3** *The New Typography was closely associated with the Modernist principles of De Stijl. This design, based on a book jacket by László Moholy-Nagy, reflects the simplified use of line and color.*

▶ **4** *Lines of type often butted up to each other or filled a panel of background color. Type was even set to read in reverse, or reflected orientations.*

1

2

3

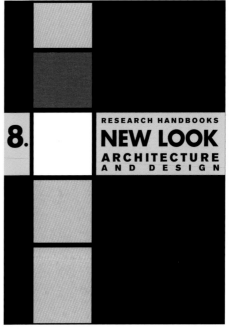

4

Piet Zwart was one of the leading proponents of the New Typography in the Netherlands. He started by following the principles of De Stijl and Dada, moving toward Constructivism with the emphasis on the diagonal, mixed with geometric shape and primary color, in an attempt to break free from the restrictions of traditional typography. He introduced the New Typography to both the public and commercial sectors through posters, catalogs, and advertisements.

Zwart was an innovator and experimenter with type, using letters and lines of text as drawing tools. The composition below is inspired by a page from a printer's booklet designed by Zwart. Letters in wildly diverse fonts and sizes stream across the page to create an exciting and very contemporary design. For Zwart, this would have been a very time-consuming exercise; thanks to the computer, complex, digitally created typographic art, making use of multiple typefaces, can now be created with minimum effort.

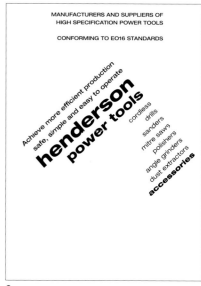

1

2

◄ **1** *Create a typical Zwart look by mixing the alignment of the text. Set some lines horizontally and some on a diagonal. To make the arrangement more flexible, first key the text into a vector drawing or page-layout application.*

◄ **2** *Select the lines to be turned diagonally and create outlines of the text, grouping the individual lines to effectively make each line a graphic element. This allows you to use the* **Align** *commands. Rotate the group to the desired angle.*

▲ **3** *Right-align the rotated text with the horizontal lines. Space the lines down the page using the* **Vertical Distribution** *command.*

▶ **4** *The colors were invariably restricted to black, red, and blue, with the white space of the paper playing a vital role. Zwart often included photography, printing the images using one or two of the flat colors. Color images can be transformed with Photoshop by first converting them to black and white and then switching the mode to* **Monotone** *or* **Duotone***, applying a single color or two hues of the same color to give slightly more depth. Overlap images and set the blending mode to* **Multiply***.*

PHOTOMONTAGE

The twenties also saw the introduction of Photomontage, a new technique introduced by the Berlin Dadaists and used for many image-based designs. The question of exactly which member invented the term has yet to be resolved—primarily because many of the montages produced at this time were collaborative efforts. That said, its five key exponents, John Heartfield, Hannah Höch, Johannes Baader, Raoul Hausmann, and George Grosz—each of whom went on to develop their own style of photomontage—all agreed that they needed a name for their work that set it apart from Cubist collages of the previous decade. And so Photomontage was born. Often created in a fairly random, anarchic style, these Dada montages were often made up of photography juxtaposed with newspaper text and were used as magazine covers and illustrations.

LAYOUT

As the first commercial color film was not introduced by the Kodak company until 1935, the Photomontage artists used black and white images, sometimes adding tints of color by hand. Pictures were assembled from different sources. Original prints were mixed with images cut from magazines and newspapers using mass-produced paper and coarse halftones, so quality generally took second place to content. This crude photographic imagery can be recreated using Photoshop color and saturation controls.

▼ *The Dada artists added type as an integral part of the montage, cutting words or individual letters from printed sources. The effect can be reproduced digitally by typing onto a tinted color background, rasterizing the text and flattening the document. Draw crude paths around words or letters. Copy the selected areas and paste onto new layers in the master montage document. The selections can then be scaled or rotated.*

▲ *Collage*, Da-Dandy, *Hannah Höch, 1919*

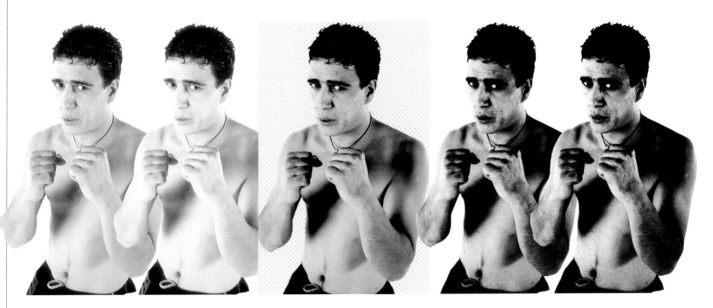

▲ For figures, collections of "bodyshots" are available on disc, or individual images can be downloaded online. These usually come with a prepared **Alpha** channel which will facilitate the selection of the figure, allowing an accurate "cutout" to be copied and pasted into a master photomontage document. Simply changing

the color mode to grayscale will not produce the required effect when using modern high-resolution digital images. A more authentic look is created by using **Image** > **Adjustment** > **Hue/Saturation** and reducing the saturation level, leaving a minimum amount of color. Further reduce the brightness and increase the

contrast. A color cast can then be added with the **Color Balance** controls, to simulate hand tinting. Newspaper print can be simulated by using the **Sketch** > **Halftone** filter with foreground color set to black and background to white. A flat color tint can then be added to a background layer and the blending mode of the original image set to **Darken**.

◄◄ Sometimes the image was cut or torn from a page, leaving some of the original background intact. An elliptical selection made in Photoshop and subsequently saved as a path will produce a rough, bitmapped edge, giving the impression of torn paper.

◄ Images were cut by hand, so perfect digital cutouts are not appropriate. For a period feel, draw quick, rough paths around the subject to replicate the effect of scissors.

PHOTOMONTAGE

METHOD

▲ Encouraging the populace to lead healthy, active lifestyles was a popular theme in magazines and advertising between the wars. Photomontage was frequently employed to promote the message. The scale and juxtaposition of the individual images often struck a slightly humorous note.

▶ This image was constructed using stock "bodyshots." Each cutout was selected, copied, and pasted into a new Photoshop layer. The **Saturation**, **Color Balance**, and **Brightness/Contrast** of each layer was adjusted to make each element appear to come from a different source.

BACKGROUND

STEP 1 Color was added in the background, either with hand-painted areas or shapes, or tinted texture derived from printed material. A De Stijl effect can be created by drawing rectangles and filling them with primary colors, each on a separate layer.

STEP 2 Arrange some of the rectangles into a linear design, then select the layers and **Edit** > **Transform** > **Rotate** them all in a single action. Adjust the position of individual layers by nudging with the arrow keys.

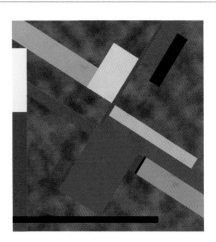

STEP 3 A mottled, hand-painted background is added behind the design by filling a layer with a chosen color and applying the **Render** > **Clouds** filter. The opacity of each of the colored panel layers can be adjusted to allow some background color to show through.

SPORT

HEALTH AND FITNESS

RECREATION

FUTURISM

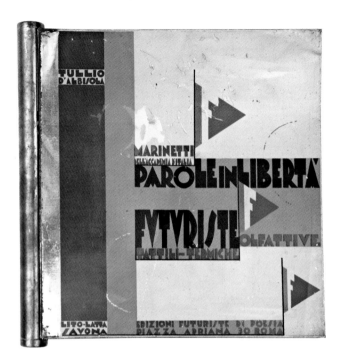

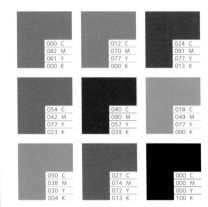

COLOR

000 C 082 M 061 Y 000 K	012 C 070 M 077 Y 000 K	024 C 091 M 077 Y 013 K
054 C 042 M 077 Y 023 K	040 C 090 M 057 Y 039 K	018 C 049 M 077 Y 000 K
050 C 038 M 030 Y 004 K	027 C 074 M 072 Y 013 K	000 C 000 M 000 Y 100 K

Many subtly different shades of red, brown, and olive green were the key Futurist colors. Marinetti mixed three or four colors on the page, for both type and backgrounds, with key words or blocks of text overprinted in black.

The first Futurist Manifesto was published in 1909, encouraging young artists to embrace modern technology, speed, the age of the machine, and war. Led by Italian writer and poet Filippo Tommaso Marinetti, Futurist artists depicted urban subjects and machinery as Cubist-inspired fragmented and faceted forms. Speed was represented by lines of force, and dynamism was created by repeating motifs and typographic elements.

Marinetti advocated the concept of "typographic architecture," to "redouble the expressive force of words." This consisted of visually exciting layouts using text set in multiple typefaces arranged on the page in different directions, and playing with scale and color, overlaying, and letterspacing. To make his enthusiasm for technology even more explicit, Marinetti sometimes used tin plate to bind his books.

Throughout the late 1920s and 1930s the Futurist style of typography was often used commercially in book, magazine, and advertising design.

FONTS

Futura Book
AaBbCcDdEeFfGgH

Helvetica Ultra Compressed
AaBbCcDdEeFfGgHhIiJjKkLlMmNnO

Trade Gothic Bold Extended
AaBbCcDdEeF

Poplar Standard
AaBbCcDdEeFfGgHhIiJjKk

The Sans Black
AaBbCcDdEeFfGgH

Marinetti's message was really "anything goes." His typefaces were generally a mixture of period standards such as Futura, with dynamic hand-drawn letterforms inspired by the machine. He sometimes used up to twenty different typefaces on a single page to ensure the visual effect of the words had as much meaning as the language itself.

▲ *Cover*, Parole In Liberta Futuriste, *Filippo Tommaso Marinetti, 1932*

▶ *Typographic Architecture in action. Type individual letters and construct words so the letters flow across or down the page. Mix extended and condensed typefaces and be creative with the scale. The aim is to create a form of "concrete poetry" in which the arrangement of the letters and words reinforces the message.*

▶ ▶ *The text was overprinted onto the colored backgrounds, resulting in a slightly transparent effect. Reducing the transparency of the type by 80 to 90% creates an authentic feel.*

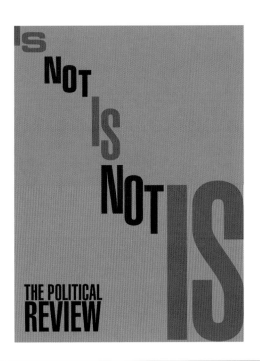

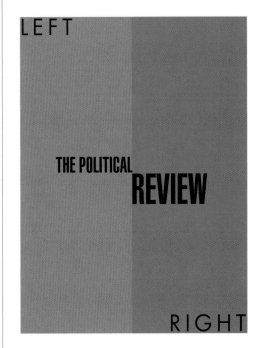

▶ *Words were often repeated to build the typographic structure of the page, with smaller text overlaying larger.*

▶ ▶ *Numbers and typographic symbols were also included if relevant. Three very contrasting typefaces have been used in this Marinetti-style menu, with subtle color combinations adding depth to the design.*

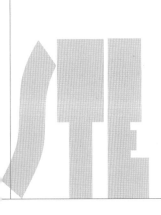

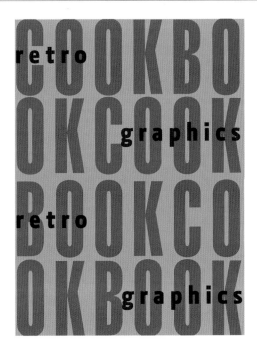

FUTURISM

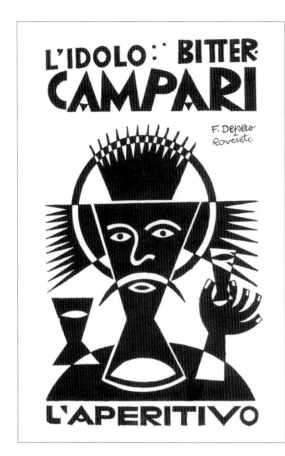

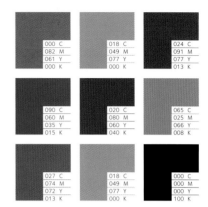

000 C 082 M 061 Y 000 K	018 C 049 M 077 Y 000 K	024 C 091 M 077 Y 013 K
090 C 060 M 035 Y 015 K	020 C 080 M 060 Y 040 K	065 C 025 M 066 Y 008 K
027 C 074 M 072 Y 013 K	018 C 049 M 077 Y 000 K	000 C 000 M 000 Y 100 K

Depero's advertising design was often monochromatic, or simply used a spot color to highlight text. Full-color work made use of the Futurist reds, browns, and ochers with an occasional bright accent of blue or aqua.

Fortunato Depero, an Italian painter, writer, sculptor, and graphic designer, was largely responsible for commercial adoption of the Futurist style. Depero was first inspired by Marinetti's Futurist manifestos, and in 1914 moved to Rome where he met Giacomo Balla. It was with Balla in 1915 that he wrote the manifesto *Futurist Reconstruction of the Universe*, which expanded upon the ideas introduced by Marinetti and other Futurists.

At the end of the 1920s, Depero spent some time in New York, where he designed covers for magazines including *The New Yorker*, *Movie Maker*, *Vanity Fair*, and *Vogue*. His commercial work included the striking advertising design for Campari pictured above, using Futurism's simplified symbolism and dynamic geometric lines. In 1927, he produced a remarkable book of examples of his own work, *Depera Futurista*.

P22 Il Futurismo Regular

P22 Il Futurismo Velocita

P22 Il Futurismo Extras

Depero's characteristic fonts and symbols were hand-drawn. Type foundry P22 has created a font set based on his original designs. The icons in the Il Futurismo Extras can be outlined and combined to recreate Depero's commercial style.

▲ *Advertising poster, Campari, Fortunato Depero, 1930*

▶ *Dynamic positioning of typographic elements, combined with geometric shapes or arrows, was common in Depero's work. When objects crossed over each other, colors were often reversed. Key in the type using a vector application, and use the* **Create Outlines** *command.* **Ungroup** *the letters to allow individual sizing and positioning. Add any required shapes using the* **Pen** *tool. A false 3-dimensional effect can be created by duplicating letter "objects" to make drop shadows. Once you are satisfied with the arrangement, select all the elements and apply the* **Pathfinder** > **Divide** *command.*

▶▶ *Add color to each new divided section. Where objects appear to overlap, change the color accordingly to create a positive/negative effect.*

▶ *Depero-style woodcut illustrations and icons are available in P22's Il Futurismo Extras font. Once selected, create outlines, turning the symbol into a vector object. It can then be simply scaled or adapted as required.*

▶▶ *Type played an important role in the overall construction of Depero's designs. Typically it was arranged both horizontally and vertically, framing an illustration, or combined with arrow symbols for emphasis and direction.*

the GREAT
MAGICIAN

1930 ❯ 1939

The Great Depression in America and subsequent economic downturn in Europe during the early thirties quickly led to a return to simple living. As the Nazis tightened their grip on Germany, the Bauhaus was finally closed for good on August 10, 1933. Many of the German designers who had pioneered the Modern movement left their homeland and emigrated to either the U.K. or the U.S. to escape. The upside of this was that the Modernist ethic soon spread to the rest of the world. 1930 saw the launch of *Advertising Arts* magazine, the weekly supplement to *Advertising & Selling*, the magazine responsible for introducing "modernistic" design to American advertising, while in 1932 Stanley Morison designed what would become one of the most widely used typefaces of the twentieth century—Times New Roman—for *The Times* of London. The following year saw a breakthrough in information design as Henry Beck produced his famous map for the London Underground. Rather than take the conventional approach, Beck simplified the Underground system down to its bare bones to create a design concept that is still going strong today.

Having emerged in France during the 1920s, the rise of Art Deco continued through the 1930s. Influenced by the costume designs of Diaghilev's Ballets Russes and the fashions of Paul Poiret, Art Deco celebrated luxury, travel, and speed with vivid colors and geometric styling. Celebrating this newfound fascination with travel and speed, advertising posters began to adopt bold silhouettes and simplified forms, exemplified by AM Cassandre's 1931 *L'Atlantique* poster, the quintessential graphic travel poster of the decade. Edward McKnight Kauffer was another of Europe's most prolific and influential advertising poster artists during this period. In architecture, too, the opening of New York's Chrysler Building, complete with its geometric Art Deco styling, epitomized this exuberant new style.

Futurism had also emerged as a design style in Italy thanks to the writer and poet Filippo Tommaso Marinetti, whose first Futurist manifesto was published in French in the Parisian newspaper *Le Figaro*. The Futurists embraced technological progress and the dynamism of the Modern Age. Their expressive typography broke all the traditional rules of layout in favor of vivid pictorials. Widely influential, Marinetti's approach led to the production of hundreds of Futurist books. One of the best known was Fortunato Depero's 1927 *Depero Futurista*, which, held together by two aluminum bolts, was a true manifesto of the machine age. Having initially made its mark as a design style during the twenties, by the thirties Futurism had also begun to influence the world of advertising, thanks to Depero's striking commercial designs for Campari. The designer even published a book, *Campari Futurist*, devoted to his advertising campaigns for the brand.

Modernist graphic design also found favor in Switzerland. The efficiency for which the Swiss were—and still are—renowned was reflected in their precise, and in many ways unique, graphic language. Characterized by its use of white space and sans-serif typefaces, proponents of the Swiss Style believed the solution to a design problem should emerge from its content. For them, clarity and order was the ultimate goal. Swiss graphic designers, such as Herbert Matter, also brought an element of vitality to their work. After studying in Paris, Matter returned to his native Switzerland, where he remained from 1932 until 1936, designing posters for the Swiss National Tourist Office. Matter understood the new approaches and techniques, such as visual organization, collage, and montage, that had arisen as a result of the Modern Movement and enthusiastically incorporated them into his work.

The end of the thirties saw the opening of the New York World's Fair, showcasing the latest designs in the streamline style by the likes of Raymond Loewy and Norman Bel Geddes; but, with the Second World War just around the corner, it wasn't long before designers found themselves with more pressing duties.

▲ *Travel poster, H. Chauffard, 1930*

ART DECO

▲ *Poster*, La Plage de Monte Carlo, *Michel Bouchard, 1933*

COLOR

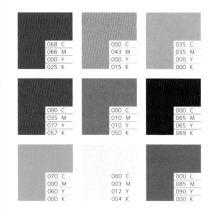

The Art Deco palette was subtle and varied, mixing the neutral hues of the 1920s with the bolder tones that emerged toward the end of the decade. Mauves, pinks, and lavenders were popular, with warmer wood tones inspired by the interior design of the period. Lipstick red offset cool greens and blues and slightly harder-edged metallic influences.

MOTIFS

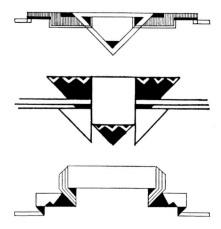

The Art Deco decorative style was drawn from geometric shapes: pyramids, obelisks, lightning bolts, and sunrays. The graphic patterns produced could be intricate in detail. It is a style perfectly suited to digital recreation, as the computer can instantly perform tasks such as duplication and rotation via simple keystroke commands.

Art Deco is the name attributed to the international style of art, design, and architecture that first emerged in Paris during the 1920s. The style was characterized by the use of angular, geometric stepped forms and bright colors. Two classic architectural examples of the Art Deco style are New York's Chrysler Building and Empire State Building, both of which were completed during the 1930s. In graphics, the term was used to refer to the many geometric designs created during this period. A strong Cubist influence, as well as elements of the Bauhaus, Secessionist, and De Stijl aesthetics, can clearly be seen in many of these designs.

Broadway

ABCDEFGHIJKLMNOPQRSTUVWXYZ
abcdefghijklmnopqrstuvwxyz
0123456789!?@#$:;""''()&%<>

Nouveau Asta

ABCDEFGHIJKLMNOPQRSTUVWXYZ
0123456789!?@#$:;""''()&%<>

Eagle

ABCDEFGHIJKLMNOPQRSTUVWXYZ
abcdefghijklmnopqrstuvwxyz

Marquee Mieux Regular

ABCDEFGHIJKLMNOPQRSTUVWXYZ
0123456789!?@#$:;""''()&%<>

Baccarat

ABCDEFGHIJKLMNOPQRSTUVWXYZ

Elisia

ABCDEFGHIJKLMNOPQRSTUVWXYZ
abcdefghijklmnopqrstuvwxyz

ITC Anna

ABCDEFGHIJKLMNOPQRSTUVWXYZ

Art Deco typefaces evolved the sans-serif fonts of the Machine Age into less austere forms with more character and panache. The geometric sans-serifs were refined to make more elegant forms with emphasized stroke contrast and abrupt junctures. These were accompanied by delicate faces with small, truncated serifs.

ART DECO

Art Deco openly and unashamedly celebrated speed, travel, and luxury, and the new and faster ocean liners and streamlined trains that made once-distant lands accessible were the ultimate symbols of Art Deco elegance and comfort. As the travel industry began to expand and competition increased, it wasn't long before the various steamship and rail companies were spending vast amounts of money commissioning contemporary artists to promote their services. The series of striking poster designs that resulted echoed this feeling, emphasizing speed and comfort as the ultimate characteristics of the modern world. One of the leading poster artists of this period was AM Cassandre, whose bold designs often condensed his subject into simple lines and angular shapes, influenced by the Cubist style pioneered by Picasso and Braque.

▲ *Poster,* Normandie, *artist unknown, late 1930s*

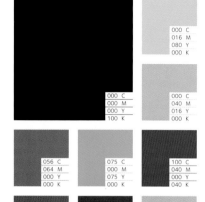

000 C / 000 M / 000 Y / 100 K	000 C / 016 M / 080 Y / 000 K
	000 C / 040 M / 016 Y / 000 K
056 C / 064 M / 000 Y / 000 K	075 C / 000 M / 075 Y / 000 K	100 C / 040 M / 000 Y / 040 K
046 C / 065 M / 077 Y / 020 K	000 C / 100 M / 080 Y / 000 K	040 C / 024 M / 000 Y / 000 K

The vessels and trains were depicted in dominant black, with highlight colors for sky, sea, and small details such as funnels.

FONTS

Rockwell Bold Condensed
ABCDEFGHIJKLMNO

Futura Extra Bold
ABCDEFGHIJKL

Avant Garde Gothic
ABCDEFGHIJKLM

Din Engschrift
ABCDEFGHIJKLMNOPQRS

Impact
ABCDEFGHIJKLMNOPQ

The travel poster tended to feature the less decorative Art Deco typefaces, often solid block capitals in medium to heavy weights, sometimes mixing condensed with roman styles. Later in the decade, a slab-serif was occasionally introduced.

▲ Text was treated in a number of different ways. Color could be alternated from one letter of a word to another; drop shadows added in color or white rather than black. Letter spacing might be removed or negative spacing introduced, highlighting the overlapping areas in another color. Headlines were generally center-aligned, at the top or base.

◀ The mode of transportation was the hero, with any imagery of the destination usually taking second place. The ships were colossal and majestic, the trains infinitely long. Exaggerated horizons and perspectives were characteristic of the travel poster, often accentuated by lines indicating speed, stolen from the Futurists. Secondary text sometimes became part of the illustration, running around the edge as a border, or creating an independent shape such as train tracks.

As most of the illustration was simplified and stylized, it is possible to create the effect by drawing geometric shapes with a **Shape** or **Pen** tool and adding flat color or graduated tints. For flexibility, always draw each new element on a new layer (see p. 84).

1930s TRAVEL POSTER

ART DECO

METHOD

The ability to digitally duplicate and flip or reflect elements makes it easy to create a "symmetrical" steamship design in the style of the classic posters by AM Cassandre. Use a photograph of a cruise liner, or one of the many published examples of the genre, as a guide.

STEP 1 *Place a vertical guide to form the center of the illustration and draw paths to outline the basic shapes of half the image. Keep detail to a minimum and remember that only two colors will be used to delineate the hull from the upper deck structure.*

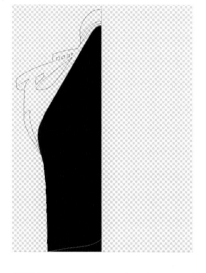

STEP 2 *Create a new layer, select the sub-path you want to fill (in this case the hull) and fill with a solid black composed of all four process colors. Duplicate this layer and apply* **Edit** *>* **Transform** *>* **Flip Horizontal***, then position the new layer on the other side of the center guide.*

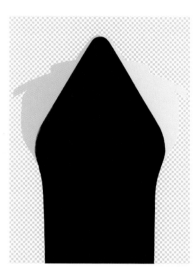

STEP 3 *Select the path delineating the upper deck area, and fill, on a new layer, with a neutral off-white color. Duplicate and flip the layer. Start creating the effect of sunlight by making the new layer several shades lighter using the* **Brightness/Contrast** *control.*

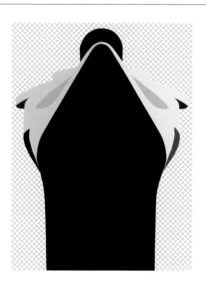

STEP 4 *Continue to build consecutive layers with each new element, duplicating and flipping each layer, until the symmetrical structure of the boat is complete.*

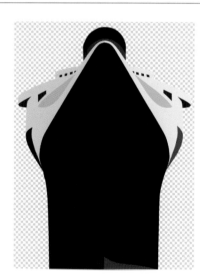

STEP 5 *Add a minimal amount of detail in the same way, including a highlight color for the stack and waterline. Adjust the brightness of the reflected layer to indicate the bowline.*

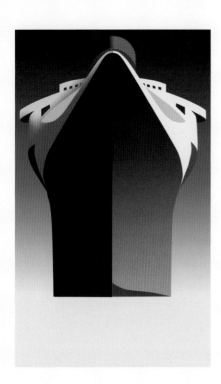

STEP 6 *Add shading to simulate the three-dimensional structure. Go back to the duplicate layer of the first section of the hull. Duplicate this layer and use the **Brightness/Contrast** control to make it considerably lighter. Choose **Layer > Layer Mask > Reveal All**, and, using the **Gradient** tool, drag a short vertical line down the center of the shape. This creates a transparent gradient revealing the original dark layer. This method can be applied to other areas to create shadow or highlight as required.*

A highlight has also been added to the tip of the prow with a soft airbrush. A reflected sunlight effect can be created by choosing the appropriate layer, selecting the existing color and filling the selection with a warmer hue.

Create the background and sea by again using two layers filled with different colors and applying a layer mask gradient to each. Wisps of smoke drifting from the stack add a touch of movement.

Add text. Here a mixture of Futura and Trade Gothic Bold Condensed is used, the main title reflecting the sunny color of the upper decks.

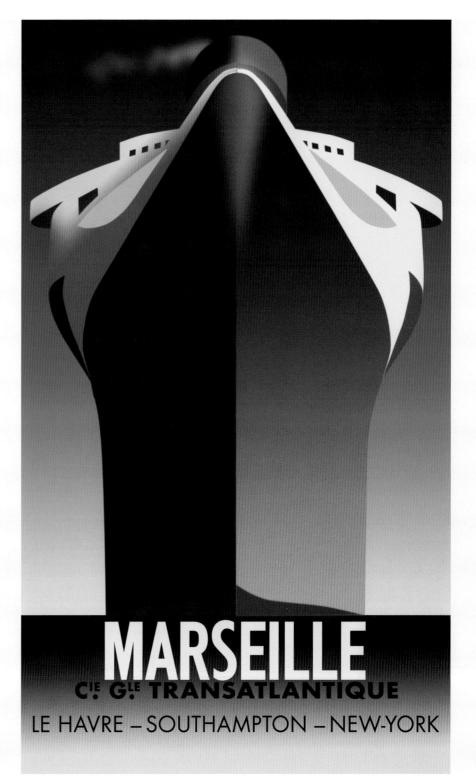

ART DECO

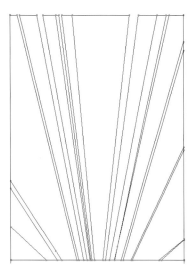

METHOD

STEP 1 *The Art Deco design style was dominated by geometric patterns. Sunbursts and zigzag motifs could be found everywhere. Draw a series of shapes using a vector application, radiating from a horizon at the base of the page.*

The bold silhouettes and dramatically simplified letterforms that characterized the Art Deco style were equally evident in the American fashion magazines of the day. By the late 1930s, many leading European designers had moved to America, each bringing his own unique style and approach. Before long, the once staid and stuffy layouts had been replaced with full-bleed imagery, machine-set sans-serif type, and asymmetrical layouts. Dr. Mehemed Fehmy Agha's work for both *Vanity Fair* and *House & Garden* led the way, while Carmel Snow's appointment as editor of *Harper's Bazaar* in 1933 and subsequent decision to employ Alexey Brodovitch as art director the following year led to nothing short of a revolution in editorial design.

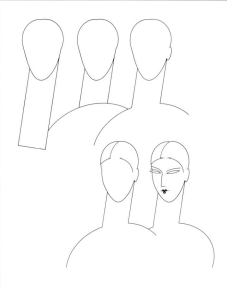

STEP 4 *Eyes were also narrowed to give them a feline quality; lipstick-red lips were often stylized, cupid-like, and unnaturally narrow. Draw the shapes freehand with the **Pen** tool and then outline or fill them with solid color.*

▲ Vogue *magazine cover, Eduardo Benito, 1926*

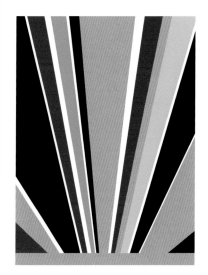

STEP 2 *Add color to the shapes from the Deco palettes (see pp. 80, 82). Mix softer hues with brighter, and include black to add contrast to the effect.*

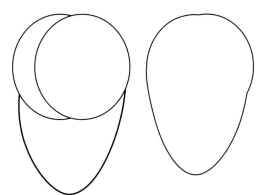

STEP 3 *It is not difficult to create a Deco "portrait" in the style of the 1930s fashion magazine. Lots of Deco-related clip-art material is available for reference. Using a vector application such as Illustrator, draw simple shapes and* **Combine** *them to make the elements. Hair was cut short, or the head covered with a scarf or tightly fitting hat, so the head can be easily constructed with circles or ellipses. The elongated neck is a rectangle and the stylized shoulders another ellipse. Once the basic form is drawn, add details such as ears, hair or hat lines, nose, and eyebrows.*

STEP 5 *Add the head elements to the background and bring some of the sunburst shapes to the front. The subject's skin and hair tones have been left neutral to create a statuesque, porcelain effect, with detail depicted by simple lines.*

STEP 6 *Color adjustment and detail has been added in Photoshop. The lines of facial detail have been softened with the* **Airbrush** *to make them look hand-drawn. Very subtle airbrushed shading has been added to create more depth. The all-important drop earrings are added to accentuate the length of the neck, and also a fan detail. Finally, a masthead is included. Choose a suitable Deco typeface and give it a two-tone color or add a drop shadow for authenticity. A two-tone effect is created by duplicating the original black text layer, changing the color of the new text layer to white, and rasterizing the type. Erase, or select and delete, sections of the white letters to reveal the black letters beneath.*

MODERNISM

Zürich and Basel were the home of several influential design schools, publishers, and printers in the 1930s, and Switzerland became an important focus for graphic designers from many countries in Europe, largely due to the pressures and imposed artistic restrictions of National Socialist policy.

Several Swiss-born designers developed their own influential styles. Designer and photographer Herbert Matter produced a series of celebrated travel posters for the Swiss National Tourist Office before emigrating to America in 1936. The posters were notable for their extreme contrasts of scale—often depicting large positive faces photomontaged against contours of mountains and skiers.

COLOR

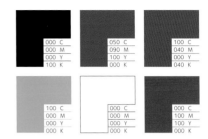

000 C
000 M
000 Y
100 K

050 C
090 M
100 Y
000 K

100 C
040 M
000 Y
040 K

100 C
000 M
000 Y
000 K

000 C
000 M
000 Y
000 K

000 C
100 M
100 Y
000 K

Matter's posters were printed by gravure, the method used for print magazines, giving the photographic images the same grainy quality. Color or hand-tinted images were combined with black-and-white or tinted monochromes. The skin tones were unnaturally dark to promote the effects of the sun, while the monochromatic backgrounds reflected the cool snow and blue skies. Red, the Swiss national color, was often used for text or as a spot highlight.

FONTS

Haettenschweiler
AaBbCcDdEeFfGgHhIiJjKkLlM

Helvetica Compressed
AaBbCcDdEeFfGgHhIiJjK

Impact
AaBbCcDdEeFfGgHhIi

Compacta Bold
AaBbCcDdEeFfGgHhIiJjKk

Eurostile Bold Condensed
AaBbCcDdEeFfGgHhIiJ

The bold, condensed, sans-serif typefaces of Matter's Swiss posters were hand-lettered, but the effect can be simulated using many modern digital fonts. The Swiss have played an important role in the development of typography. Though not launched until 1960, the classic Helvetica was created by a Swiss typographer, Max Miedinger.

▲ *Poster,* Pontresina, *Herbert Matter, 1934*

STEP 1 *Select a foreground image with a suitably positive expression. Many examples can be found in royalty-free image libraries. If the subject is wearing sunglasses, you are unlikely to find true styles of the era, but make sure the design of the glasses is relatively classical.*

STEP 2 *Remove the unwanted background by painting a mask or drawing a path around the subject. This image has been flipped to create a more positive effect.*

STEP 5 *Find a mountain scene for the background image, preferably displaying a good contrast between snow and sky. Convert the image grayscale, then change the mode to mono or duotone, selecting a blue (or two shades of blue for a duotone to give slightly more depth), before reverting to CMYK.*

STEP 6 *Combine the two images on separate layers to allow positioning and final adjustments. The subject's long hair has been removed to conform with the style of the period. Text has been added, positioned at an angle and colored with a* **Linear Blend** *and* **Drop Shadow***, which is typical of the Matter style. A small figure of a skier emphasizes the contrasts of scale.*

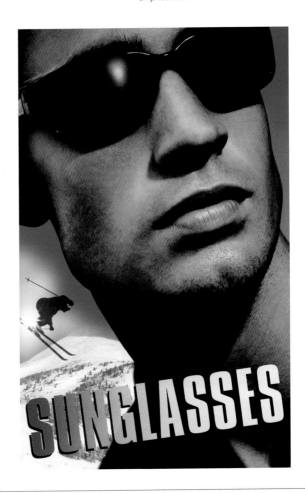

STEP 3 *Adjust the colors by reducing the brightness and saturation and increasing the contrast to create the exaggerated suntan tones. You may need to experiment with the* **Color Balance***, increasing the red as necessary. A* **Lens Flare** *highlight has also been added to the glasses.*

STEP 4 *For a more authentic color simulation, change the mode to grayscale and then apply a* **Duotone** > **Tritone** *using black and shades of red. When you are satisfied with the result, convert the image back to CMYK. The highlight on the glasses has been modified using the* **Airbrush** *tool.*

MODERNISM

COLOR

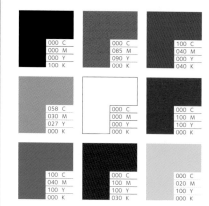

000 C 000 M 000 Y 100 K	000 C 085 M 090 Y 000 K	100 C 040 M 000 Y 040 K
058 C 030 M 027 Y 000 K	000 C 000 M 000 Y 000 K	000 C 100 M 100 Y 000 K
100 C 040 M 100 Y 000 K	000 C 100 M 100 Y 030 K	000 C 020 M 100 Y 000 K

The color emphasis depended largely on the political movement being promoted. In the Soviet Union and China, red was the obvious dominant theme. In Italy and Germany, black presided over reds, yellow, and orange. Blue skies, maps, workers' shirts, and military uniforms made it possible to add the key notes.

FONTS

Futura Extra Bold
AaBbCcDdEeFfG

Futura Extra Bold Condensed
AaBbCcDdEeFfGgHh

Futurismo Regular
ABCDEFGHIJKLMNN

Gill Sans Extra Condensed Bold
AaBbCcDdEeFfGgHhIiJjKkLlMmNnOoPp

The Sans Black caps
ABCDEFGHIJKLMNO

The Italians employed the angular block capitals derived from the Futurists, with spiked ascenders and a compressed "s"; German propaganda sometimes reverted to the gothic Blackletter style. But on the whole, the European political poster used Modernist sans-serif typography, rather than the more decorative commercial Art Deco typefaces.

Viewed from a graphic-design perspective, the Spanish Civil War, which took place between 1936 and 1939, spawned a whole range of stunning visual imagery. Although much propaganda art and heroic realism was confined to socialist nations, propaganda posters (such as the one shown here supporting the Popular Front government against the backing of the Nationalist Spanish troops by Germany and Italy) were deployed by both Nationalists and Republicans to recruit people to their cause. Similarly, periodicals that appeared throughout Europe, especially those in liberal democratic states such as Britain and France, used photographs of the war for their own propaganda ends.

▲ *Poster,* Kion vi faras por eviti tion, *artist unknown, 1937*

▲ Political propaganda in both Europe and the Soviet Union utilized certain common elements, the clenched fist being particularly prevalent. The fist was depicted in various stages of stylization, from figurative to abstract, sometimes isolated, sometimes attached to an outstretched arm, but always given exaggerated strength and power. The other common icons were the flag and the face, with chiseled features set in a heroic expression.

▼ Emphasizing the message through perspective was a trick used frequently by the Italian Fascist propaganda artists. Introduced by the Futurists in the quest to represent speed, text was often represented as if applied to monumental architectural structures or roads zooming toward an infinite horizon. The distortion tools available in both vector and bitmap software make this effect simple to achieve.

▲ An exhibition poster demonstrating generic political propaganda symbolism, created using Illustrator. The essence of the style would be appropriate for either 1930s Soviet or European propaganda art. The angular forms of the simplified figures, drawn with a **Pen** tool using only straight lines, emphasize the curving sweep of the flag.

MODERNISM

Heroic Realism was a style of propaganda art used primarily in the Soviet Union (Soviet Socialist Realism) and Germany (Nazi Heroic Realism) during the 1930s. At around the time that Hitler came to power in Germany, modern sans-serif typefaces were banned and modern art was replaced with classically heroic art. The resulting political propaganda posters played a role in the Nazi rise to power. Soviet Socialist Realism, meanwhile, rejected the "bourgeois influence on art" in favor of photography and new typographic layouts. The use of this visual style was not confined to propaganda in dictatorships or socialist nations, however. It was also used during the Spanish Civil War and by Western democracies to promote their aims in time of war.

DESIGN

THE FIGHT STARTS IN THE FIELDS

▲ *In the Soviet Union, the 1930s propaganda poster delivered an optimistic message. Posters were designed to portray the successes of the economic plan and record the achievements of the proletariat. The images were of plants, fields, collective farms, power stations, construction sites, and people proudly at work. Photography played an increasingly important role, with black-and-white images of the heroic worker often set against a hand-rendered flag or factory backdrop. Pictures of women were often used to personify the strength and sense of duty of the Soviet workforce. The common denominator was the positive expression, heads upturned toward a better future.*

*Contemporary photographic images can be given a period feel by applying a **Film Grain** filter, or adding some **Noise** such as **Dust and Scratches**. The farm girl above was taken from a turn-of-the-century color illustration and given a photographic interpretation by applying a **Halftone** filter. Silhouettes of workers on tractors are another common feature of the Soviet poster.*

▲ *Poster,* Come and join our collective farm, comrade!, *Vera Korableva, 1930*

◀▼ Statues provide the perfect resource for the "heroic" poster. The angle of view was always from below, looking up to the hero, and as most statues are sited on plinths, photography will provide the correct perspective. A background has been created using a colored gradient with a touch of texture added to age it. The **Paint Daubs** filter has been applied to the statue image and the blending mode set to **Color Burn**. The flag is hand-drawn and filled with solid color. Lastly, text is added and **Warped** to follow the lines of the flag.

◀▼ Another variation on the statue theme. A path has been drawn around the stone figure, to allow the removal of unwanted background. To simulate a painted effect, the **Paint Daubs** filter has been applied to the figure and then the color boosted using the **Hue/Saturation** control. Hue is reduced to highlight red, and saturation increased to 90% to effectively color the darker shadow areas. A gradient background and a simple text message complete the image.

Esenit Praestrud Sstie Velis!

KNOW YOUR RIGHTS

MODERNISM

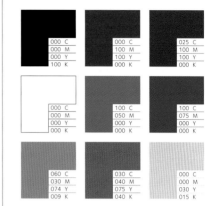

The "corporate" colors of red and blue, used in the London Underground logo, were reinforced in the advertising. These basics were complemented by subtler Deco hues of green and brown. Black was also used extensively both for text and imagery. As the campaigns became more successful, they were dominated by illustrations using a much wider color palette.

In the 1930s, London Transport was a keen supporter of contemporary art and design and commissioned a number of high-profile artists and designers to create publicity posters for its network. Many of the best known of these examples were commissioned by Frank Pick, who was appointed managing director in 1933. Pick wanted London Transport to inspire and educate those who used its services and his ambitious list of prospective artists reflected this. Many passengers looked forward to seeing the latest works by these eminent designers and Pick also organized exhibitions of these posters in the booking office at Charing Cross Station. Edward McKnight Kauffer was one of the first artists to be commissioned by Pick and others soon followed, including Graham Sutherland, Paul Nash, László Moholy-Nagy, and Man Ray.

Frank Pick commissioned Edward Johnston to design the original Underground "Bullseye" logo. It has been one of the most successful trademarks ever. Updated over the years by subtle changes to the font, it is still in use today.

▲ *Stylized abstractions of elements such as clock faces were used to encourage the public to make use of the Underground at certain times for specific purposes. Dynamic, Futurist-inspired designs incorporated references to the circular logo.*

▶ *Cubist forms derived from the company logo were used as often as possible; both the archer's arm and quiver cleverly reinforce the message. The arrow symbol was widespread, especially the indented arrows either side of panels acting as rules or banners. These elements are easy to recreate using vector drawing software.*

FONTS

The Underground was a pioneer of integrated design strategies. Edward Johnston designed the sans-serif block-letter alphabet that was used for all the station signs and information notices. The Modernist design exerted a huge influence on English typography. A digital version of Johnston's original is produced by P22 type foundry.

Johnston Underground

ABCDEFGHIJKLMNOPQRSTUVWXYZ
0123456789!?@#$:;"")(&%<>

MODERNISM

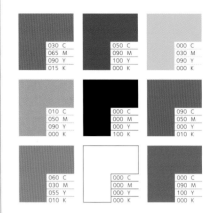

Purvis's illustrations were reduced to a limited number of strong bold colors, punctuated with spot areas of black and highlights of white. The posters designed to promote train travel to the sunshine often had skin tones rendered in exaggerated dark hues.

The graphic style of Tom Purvis is typical of this period, and relies on dramatic simplification of form and bold cutout blocks of color. This was a style perfectly suited to the large-scale advertising images used in the U.K. by railway companies and seaside resorts, being eye-catching and relatively cheap to produce. Purvis was contracted to the LNER (London & North Eastern Railway) and produced a series of impressive designs throughout the 1920s and 1930s. He became one of the first Royal Designers for Industry in 1936 and by the end of the decade was described as the "biggest name in British commercial design."

FONTS

Gill Sans Regular
AaBbCcDdEeFfGgHh

Gill Sans Light
AaBbCcDdEeFfGgHh

Gill Sans Condensed
AaBbCcDdEeFfGgHhIiJjKkLlMm

Futura Medium
AaBbCcDdEeFfGgH

Avenir 65 Medium
AaBbCcDdEeFfGg

ITC Avant Garde Gothic Book
AaBbCcDdEeFfGg

The unadorned clean lines of the Gothic sans-serif faces were the Purvis trademark. The effect can be created today using digital versions of fonts such as Gill Sans, originally designed in 1928 by Eric Gill, and used extensively in advertising and book jacket design during the 1930s.

▲ *LNER travel poster,* East Coast Joys, *Tom Purvis, 1932*

STEP 1 *Choose a suitable image to deconstruct. If a figure is required, try to use clothing that might reflect the period, or could be easily adapted. Modern dress is an immediate giveaway.*

STEP 2 *Remove the detail from the photographic image by running one of the many Photoshop filters. In this case the* **Paint Daubs** *filter was applied, followed by* **Poster Edges***.*

STEP 3 *The resulting image was opened in Illustrator and* **Live Trace** *applied. Choose a level setting of between 6 and 10 colors to simplify the trace. Expand the trace to create vector outlines.*

STEP 4 *Now the vector shapes can be selected, grouped, and have color applied. Lose as much detail as possible. Clean horizon lines can be created by simply drawing a rectangle and applying color. Unwanted areas of detail should be deleted.*

STEP 5 *The final choice of color is important to correctly mimic the style. Select strong, contrasting hues, using one or two predominant areas of flat color. The image has been further simplified by reducing the total number of colors to eight. Final subtle changes can be made to the vector image. Here the arm holding the telltale phone has been replaced and all the detail from the model's clothing removed. Freehand shapes to indicate waves have been added to create a shoreline that is typical of Purvis's style.*

THE JOYS OF THE SEASIDE
travel by TRAIN

MODERNISM

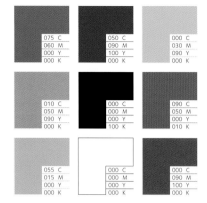

075 C	050 C	000 C
060 M	090 M	030 M
000 Y	100 Y	090 Y
000 K	000 K	000 K

010 C	000 C	090 C
050 M	000 M	050 M
090 Y	000 Y	000 Y
000 K	100 K	010 K

055 C	000 C	000 C
015 M	000 M	090 M
000 Y	000 Y	100 Y
000 K	000 K	000 K

The machines were usually depicted in red, symbolizing power. The Alpine backgrounds either merged with the sky in a single blue hue, or worked as a dramatic contrast using deep purple mountains as backdrops set against vivid skies of yellow or cyan.

During the Art Deco era, the automobile was seen as sleek and powerful, the very epitome of modernity. The Swiss poster artists of the 1930s embraced the portrayal of speed wholeheartedly and many of their most notable designs were devoted to the car. Taking inspiration from the Futurists, realism and detail were superseded by emotion. The emphasis was placed on the portrayal of speed, exaggerating the shape of the machine and distorting it with blurred lines to indicate power and motion.

Haettenschweiler
AaBbCcDdEeFfGgHhIiJjKkLlM

Helvetica Ultra Compressed
AaBbCcDdEeFfGgHhIiJjKkLlMmNn

Helvetica Black Condensed Oblique
AaBbCcDdEeFfGgHhI

Trade Gothic Bold Condensed No20 Oblique
AaBbCcDdEeFfGgHhIiJj

Insignia Alternate
AaBbCcDdEeFfGg

Futura Black BT
AaBbCcDdEeFfGgH

P22 Johnston Underground
ABCDEFGHIJKLMN

Strong geometric sans-serif faces are typical of Swiss design. The "speed" poster often used condensed or oblique versions or individual elegant hybrids of classic fonts, such as Futura.

▲ *Advertising poster, Switzerland, 1934*

STEP 1 *Classic cars still hold a romantic fascination and images can be easily found from royalty-free or clip-art libraries. Most of these images are static product shots, but the simulation of motion can be quickly created using Photoshop.*

STEP 2 *Remove much of the photographic detail by applying the **Paint Daubs** filter. This creates a painterly effect. Experiment with the settings before committing the filter; some of the detail should be retained.*

STEP 3 *Duplicate the paint daubs layer and use the **Smudge** tool to add a hint of motion distortion to certain areas. Smudge against the orientation of the vehicle, and concentrate on the extremities, such as the wheels, mudguards, and road shadows. Set the blending mode of this layer to **Overlay**.*

STEP 4 *Duplicate the original layer again, positioning it above the overlay layer. Change the blending mode to **Linear Dodge**. This has the effect of burning out the lighter areas, including the background (depending on the tonal color of the background in the original).*

STEP 5 *Now add some speed blur. Duplicate the original layer yet again and apply a **Motion Blur**. Make sure the angle of the blur is the same as the direction of the car and the strength is set to between 700 and 998 pixels.*

STEP 6 *As we only want the tail of the blur, delete the unwanted areas with a soft eraser, or hide them by making a layer mask and using the **Gradient** tool dragged in the direction of motion. This method allows you to adjust the amount of blur.*

METHOD CONT.

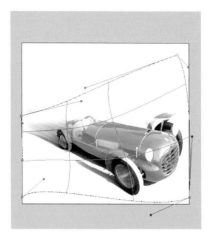

STEP 7 *Make an elliptical selection of the dominant wheels and copy the selection to a new layer. Apply a* **Radial Blur** *of 2 to 3 pixels to simulate rotation. When you are satisfied with the blurring effects, flatten the image to make a single layer.*

STEP 8 *Apply a distortion using* **Edit > Transform > Warp**. *Pull the handles and intersection points to create an exaggerated perspective. The car can be unnaturally elongated to accentuate the sense of movement.*

STEP 9 *Further minor adjustments can be made once the* **Warp** *is applied. The angle of the car may need altering for maximum impact.*

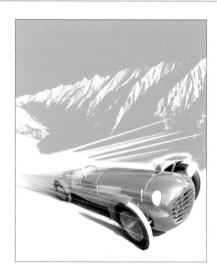

STEP 10 *Select a suitable background image. Adjust the* **Brightness/Contrast** *if necessary and make it monochrome using* **Image > Adjustments > Threshold**. *The areas of black or shadow can be selected and filled with any chosen color.*

STEP 11 *Copy the background image to the car file and position it. A soft* **Eraser** *or an* **Airbrush** *loaded with white will create a hand-drawn "halo" around the car to avoid making an accurate fit.*

STEP 12 *Add the speed lines that are typical of the period. Create two new layers, one above the car and one below. Use the* **Pen** *tool to draw spikes radiating from a perspective point behind the car. Save as* **Paths** *and fill with white. Soften the edges by applying a slight blur.*

STEP 13 *The opacity of the speed lines can be reduced on the foreground layer. Add the final touches. A ground, or road color has been placed on a new layer below the car, loosely painted with a* **Brush** *tool. More speed lines have been created over this layer. A basic silhouette of a driver has been painted by hand with a soft* **Airbrush** *and* **Motion Blur** *applied. Add the text when all else is complete.*

21ST INTERNATIONAL

FESTIVAL
OF SPEED

GENEVA   12.13.14. AUGUST 2008

MODERNISM

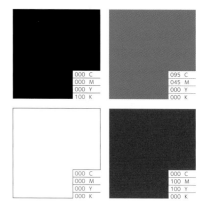

000 C	095 C
000 M	045 M
000 Y	000 Y
100 K	000 K

000 C	000 C
000 M	100 M
000 Y	100 Y
000 K	000 K

Beall montaged black-and-white photographic images of ordinary citizens at work or in the home with geometric patterns made in the colors of the national flag. Stripes and dots represented the labor force of America, collectively engaged in national improvement.

FONTS

Compacta Bold
AaBbCcDdEeFfGgHhIiJjKkLl

Impact
AaBbCcDdEeFfGgHhI

Helvetica Extra Black Condensed
AaBbCcDdEeFfGgHhI

Franklin Gothic Heavy
AaBbCcDdEeFfGg

Stencil
ABCDEFGHIJKLMN

Strong, solid sans-serif faces or industrial-looking stencil typography was used to convey the simple messages composed of few, easily understood words for a mass appeal. Sometimes the image alone was enough to convey the message.

President Roosevelt's *New Deal* economic program, introduced to combat the crisis of the Depression, included a Works Progress Administration (WPA) that commissioned graphic designers to produce information posters dedicated to the public good. Among the most renowned of the hundreds of WPA posters created by small studios around the country, was a series by Lester Beall for the Rural Electrification Administration, intended to increase public awareness of the Department of Agriculture.

Beall was one of the first American designers to incorporate European Modernist ideas into his work. His use of strong symbolic color is reminiscent of the Bauhaus, while the positioning of simple headlines (designed to grab the attention of people with limited reading skills) echoed the Soviet Constructivists.

▲ *Poster for the Rural Electrification Administration, Lester Beall, 1941*

STEP 1 *Public information posters promote good practice such as health and safety in the workplace or learning new skills. Royalty-free images of industry and education subjects can be found from stock image libraries.*

STEP 2 *Save a second copy of the original color image and change the mode to* **Grayscale***. Adjust the brightness and contrast to make denser blacks and brighter highlights. Copy the grayscale image as a new layer into the original color file.*

STEP 3 *On a new layer, create the solid color background. This can be painted with a hard* **Brush** *directly onto the layer, using the original image as a guide, or painted on a mask layer and subsequently filled with the required color. Alternatively, the areas to be filled can be selected with the* **Magic Wand** *tool while holding down the Shift key.*

STEP 4 *To give the image a period look, add a pale color overlay tint of black or yellow. Do this on a separate layer below the background color layer you have just made.*

STEP 5 *Create a suitable "pattern" image of stripes, dots, or stars (this is easily done using vector shapes in Illustrator, using the* **Duplicate** *and* **Align** *commands). Copy the pattern into the Photoshop file, either as a rasterized layer, or as a path that can be filled with color.*

DEPARTMENT OF TRADE AND INDUSTRY

▲ ▶ *Two versions of the Beall style with text added.*

RADIO

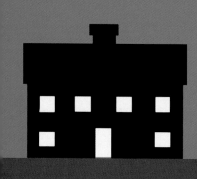

RURAL ELECTRIFICATION ADMINISTRATION

1940 > 1949

From the Second World War that raged for the first half of the decade to the first supersonic flight that took place in 1947, the forties were a decade of contrasts. America was just emerging from the Great Depression, and was reluctant to enter into an expensive foreign war. This all changed on December 7, 1941 with the Japanese attack on Pearl Harbor. The suddenness of the war, combined with the battle on two fronts, meant that the U.S. government had a difficult job reaching the public and convincing them of the need to fight. In June 1942, President Roosevelt set up the Office of War Information (OWI) to communicate the war message across a range of media. This included commissioning a range of illustrators and designers to produce graphic information. The resulting war graphics ranged from the most amateur cartoons to brilliant poster art touching on all aspects of wartime life.

An inexpensive and immediate means of communication, the poster was the perfect way to deliver messages during the war. In addition to providing a means of communication, posters also brought a much-needed spirit of community. As the OWI stated, "We want to see posters on fences, on the walls of buildings, on village greens, on boards in front of the City Hall and the Post Office, in hotel lobbies, in the windows of vacant stores—not limited to the present neat conventional frames which make them look like advertising, but shouting at people from unexpected places with all the urgency this war demands." A further message stated: "Ideally, it should be possible to post America every night. People should wake up to find a visual message everywhere, like new snow." By the mid-forties, however, as the war drew to a close and millions of troops were demobilized, wartime needs were put aside in favor of a return to civilian society.

In magazines, graphic design took pole position during the postwar period and this is often referred to as a "golden age" of magazine design. That said, only a handful of well-designed American magazines were published during this period. *Fortune, Vogue,* and *Harper's Bazaar* enjoyed little competition. Alexey Brodovitch, arguably one of the most talented designers of his time, honed his skills in editorial design as the decade progressed. As art director at *Harper's Bazaar* from 1934 until 1958, Brodovitch pioneered a new approach to magazine design through his clear, open designs, love of white space, and sharp type. Likewise, Alexander Liberman, who took over as art director of *Vogue* in 1943, and Cipe Pineles, the first woman to be allowed membership in the New York Art Director's Club, both made major contributions to editorial design during the forties.

Pulp magazines were also commonplace in the U.S. during the forties. These inexpensive fiction magazines were printed on newspaper pulp, hence the name, and were the successor to the "penny dreadfuls" of the nineteenth century. Although produced very cheaply, pulp magazines were renowned for their strong cover designs.

Paul Rand, whose work included advertising and book jackets, as well as annual reports, posters, and typefaces, was another influential designer to emerge during the forties as a result of his innovative approach to modern design. In 1946, Rand published his own monograph/manifesto under the title *Thoughts on Design.*

By the end of the decade, many countries were still counting their losses after such a long and bloody battle. With many major cities in ruins, the task of regeneration seemed almost too daunting to comprehend. But it wouldn't be long before the world began to look to the future once more, with a little help from the design industry.

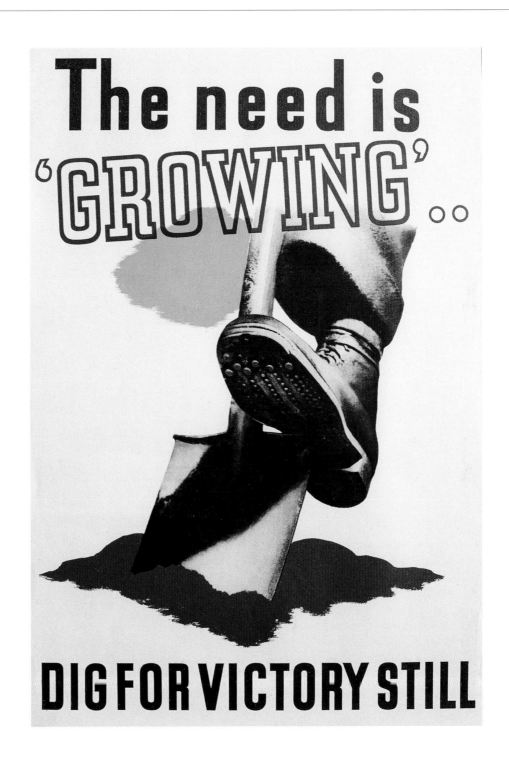

▲ *Public information poster, Ministry of Agriculture and Fisheries, c.1941*

MID-CENTURY MODERN

During the forties, editorial design in the U.S. was really coming into its own, adopting a more informal approach to organizing space. Paul Rand was one of the first designers to initiate this new independent American approach to design (often referred to as the New York School) that advocated the open expression and clear presentation of ideas. A keen proponent of Modernism, Rand firmly believed that type should be utilized to carry a message rather than solely as decoration. Between 1936 and 1941, he was art director of *Esquire* and *Apparel Arts* magazines, and from 1938 to 1945 created covers for *Direction*, a bimonthly arts and culture magazine. These covers broke with the tradition of American magazine design and cemented Rand's legendary status within the realms of contemporary design.

METHOD

Rand famously incorporated witty imagery into his designs. In this example, two images have been sourced from a stock collection. The desired pose could not be found in a single image, so elements from both were combined.

COLOR

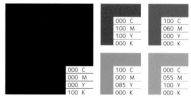

White space was a key element in Rand's work. Text was printed in black and primary spot colors were added to illustrations and photographic images. Rand introduced larger areas of primary color in his magazine covers, and his later work featured black as the dominant background theme.

FONTS

Bodoni

AaBbCcDdEeFfG

Bodoni Bold Condensed

AaBbCcDdEeFfGgHhIi

▲ *Advertisement, Paul Rand, 1946*

STEP 1 *Copy and paste right and left legs into separate layers in a new Photoshop document. Use the* **Pen** *tool to draw paths, and rotate each layer, positioning the legs in a realistic pose.*

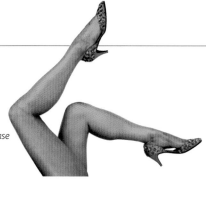

STEP 2 *Add color as a spot solid with the black image overprinted as a halftone. Save the document using a new name, and go to* **Image** *>* **Mode** *>* **Grayscale** *— do not check the* **Flatten Image** *option. Now copy and paste (or drag) the two grayscale layers back into the original color document.*

STEP 3 *Select the original color leg layers and make a duplicate layer of each. Using the* **Image** *>* **Adjustments** *>* **Brightness/ Contrast** *control, reduce the brightness by 100% and increase the contrast by 100%. This creates a black shape that can easily be selected and filled with a new flesh/tan hue.*

STEP 4 *Position both the previously created monochrome leg layers over the new color layers and change the layer blending mode to* **Multiply***.*

STEP 5 *Select the shoes by drawing a path round each, copying and pasting into new layers above the previous two.* **Desaturate** *the color and increase the contrast as necessary.*

balancing
the budget
to allow you
to buy
life's
little
luxuries
is a tricky
business...

we can help
you manage
your account
to make life
just that
little bit
more special

CAPITALBANK

STEP 6 *Choose two appropriate images to make up the "balancing" composite. This advertisement calls for female-oriented luxury goods, so a handbag and bottle of perfume have been selected from an image library. Position the two objects at jaunty angles above each other, pivoting on the topmost shoe.*

STEP 7 *Add text around both sides of the composite image, in keeping with the witty nature of the design. Rand often used Bodoni, especially in its condensed form. He was also one of the first designers to incorporate a trademark as an essential design element. White space is important in Rand's work, so make sure the composite image is not cropped too tightly.*

MID-CENTURY MODERN

LEND TO DEFEND HIS RIGHT TO BE FREE
BUY NATIONAL SAVINGS CERTIFICATES

Magazine illustrations, advertisements, and government information posters, published during and shortly after the Second World War, offer a fascinating insight into social attitudes of the time. The war may have ended in the U.K., but the government was keen to uphold the nation's wartime spirit and aid its future prosperity through the ongoing production of public information posters. With their strong, bold imagery and direct text, these posters were all about raising morale at a difficult time for Britain.

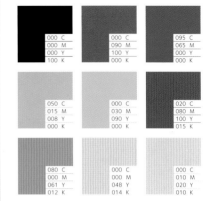

000 C 000 M 000 Y 100 K	000 C 090 M 100 Y 000 K	095 C 065 M 000 Y 000 K
050 C 015 M 008 Y 000 K	000 C 030 M 090 Y 000 K	020 C 080 M 100 Y 015 K
080 C 000 M 061 Y 012 K	000 C 000 M 048 Y 014 K	000 C 010 M 020 Y 010 K

Colors tended toward more sedate hues, possibly in an attempt to calm the nation's nerves. Text was often reversed out of solid black. To keep the cost of print production to a minimum, colors were sometimes restricted to only two or three.

FONTS

Bureau Grotesque Three Seven
ABCDEFGHIJKLMNOPQ

Impact
AaBbCcDdEeFfGgHhI

Gill Sans Bold
AaBbCcDdEeFfGg

Nivea Bold
ABCDEFGHIJKLM

Avenir Black
AaBbCcDdEeFfGg

Freestyle script
AaBbCcDdEeFfGgHhIiJjKkLl

The trend for clean, strong sans-serif typography prevailed after the war, occasionally complemented by a more frivolous script or handwritten style.

   ▲ *Poster, National Savings Committee, Tom Purvis, c.1941*

STEP 1 *The key element of the public information poster was illustration. To recreate the style, start by looking through stock photo libraries. You can get lucky and find an image that has an appropriate period feel.*

STEP 2 *Start the process by applying the* **Artistic** > **Dry Brush** *filter. Here we used a brush size of 10, Detail 10, and Texture1. A little* **Surface Blur** *can be added to disguise any obvious photographic detail.*

KEEP 'EM HEALTHY
DRINK MILK

STEP 3 *Boost the colors by selecting* **Image** > **Adjustments** > **Hue/Saturation** *and increasing the color saturation by 50 to 60%. Increase the contrast to strengthen the exaggerated shadow tones. Extra red has been lightly airbrushed onto the cheeks.*

STEP 4 *Duplicate the original layer and apply the* **Artistic** > **Graphic Pen** *filter to create hand-drawn background shadow detail. Paint a mask over the subject or simply erase the subject on this shadow layer. Set the layer blending mode to* **Darken**.

STEP 5 *Intensify the blacks using the* **Image** > **Adjustments** > **Curves** *control. Text often became an integral part of the final image by setting it inside a solid black panel, using color, or reversing it out in white.*

MID-CENTURY MODERN

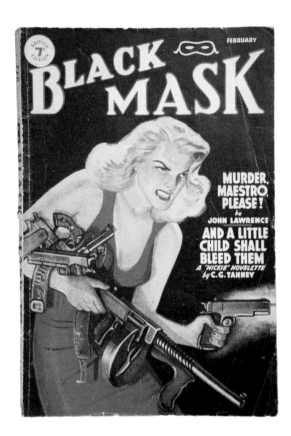

MASTHEADS

Pulp magazines—or "pulp fiction," as they became known—were widely published in America between the 1920s and the 1950s. Pulps covered a range of genres from detective and mystery titles to sci-fi, adventure, horror, and the occult, and are best remembered for their torrid cover illustrations. Impact was everything, and these lurid jackets, with their traditionally drawn characters that almost jumped off the page, fine linework, and illustrated typography became part of forties Americana. This issue of *Black Mask* was designed by Rafael DeSoto, one of the era's great pulp cover illustrators. For *Black Mask*, DeSoto's work was characterized by his use of very dark backgrounds and shadowing, and his reduction of each cover scene to a close-up, to avoid cluttering the background.

Pulp fiction mastheads or titles were varied in style, but all shared the "comic book" vernacular. Commonly drawn by hand, the words were distorted by perspective or warped into arcs and ellipses. Bright colors, drop shadows, outlined letters, and exploding sunbursts were all employed to catch the reader's eye on the bookstands.

▲ Black Mask, *Rafael DeSoto, 1942*

▼ There are many sources for high-resolution model poses. These include books with CD collections such as *500 Model Poses*, or Web sites (for example, www.photoposes.com) where collections of poses are categorized by gender, occupation, or activity, and which offer the facility to purchase and download individual images. A common theme for the pulp novel was what were regarded at the time as raunchy images of wanton women. Photoposes.com includes a number of "pin-up" poses with appropriate period dress.

1

2

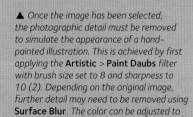

3

4

▲ Once the image has been selected, the photographic detail must be removed to simulate the appearance of a hand-painted illustration. This is achieved by first applying the **Artistic** > **Paint Daubs** filter with brush size set to 8 and sharpness to 10 (2). Depending on the original image, further detail may need to be removed using **Surface Blur**. The color can be adjusted to give a more authentic, slightly unnatural painted feel by adjusting the **Image** > **Adjustments** > **Hue/Saturation** control to boost the reds and yellows. Increasing the contrast also helps the effect (3). If the image is still looking too photographic, apply the **Blur More** filter in gradual increments until the desired result is achieved (4).

METHOD CONT.

▲ There is still too much photographic detail in the soft folds of the dress. Duplicate the layer, and remove the subject's legs with the **Eraser**. Add a **Layer Mask** and use the **Gradient** tool to make a soft gradient, removing the top part of the body. Apply more **Surface Blur** or the **Noise** > **Median** filter to remove as much detail as necessary to make the folds look hand-painted. Increasing the contrast will add to the effect.

▲ The lower part of the background was constructed using a stock photo of a city skyline. With black and white selected in the color palette for background and foreground, apply the **Artistic** > **Stamp** filter. This creates a silhouette that is then softened by applying a little **Gaussian Blur**. Duplicate and distort this layer using **Edit** > **Scale** and stretch it vertically to exaggerate the height of the buildings. Select the black area and add a new color.

▲ Type the title onto a new layer, select a fill color, and apply an outline. Experiment with various distortion effects. The individual letters or words can be selected and treated separately. **Edit** > **Skew**, **Distort** or **Perspective** can be used to recreate period styles.

▶ *The final composite image. Another stock photo of a starry night sky has been used as a background, after applying the* **Noise** > **Median** *filter. A soft outer glow has been applied to the model and a more intense outer glow to the city skyline layer. Detail is added to make the piece more authentic in the form of a price roundel and cover lines.*

▼ *The subjects of the pulp fiction covers of the 1940s typically held cigarettes. This particular pose was chosen as the model's hand was perfectly positioned to accommodate one. A simple rectangular shape is drawn, filled with a white/black gradient and rotated to the desired angle. The section of the shape obscuring the second finger has been erased.*

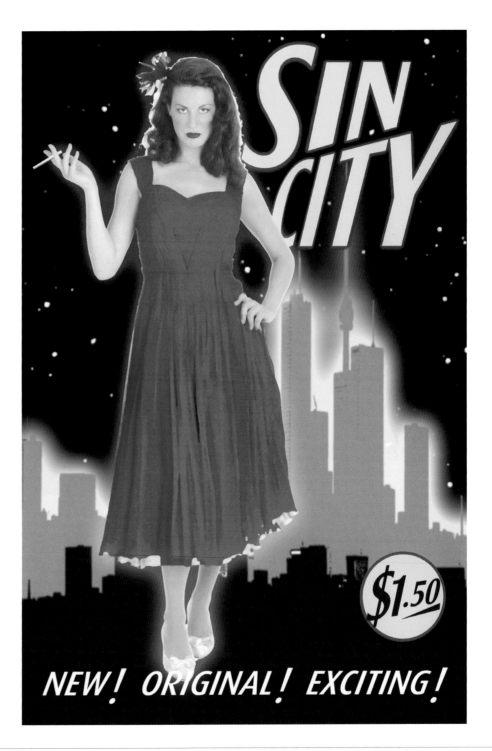

SWISS INTERNATIONAL

By the end of the Second World War, a new graphic style had begun to emerge from Switzerland and Germany. The Swiss School or the International Typographic Style, as it was also known, was renowned for its clean, functional, and objective approach to design. Sans-serif typography expressed the style's progressive spirit while the use of mathematical grids provided structure. One of the pioneers of the movement was Max Bill, an architect, artist, and designer who had studied at the Bauhaus from 1927 to 1929. Bill also embraced the idea of *art concrete*—the construction of paintings from pure, mathematically exact visual elements, such as planes and colors. As he stated in 1949: "It is possible to develop an art largely on the basis of mathematical thinking."

COLOR

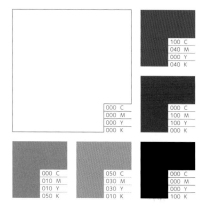

100 C
040 M
000 Y
040 K

000 C
000 M
000 Y
000 K

000 C
100 M
100 Y
000 K

000 C
010 M
010 Y
050 K

050 C
030 M
030 Y
010 K

000 C
000 M
000 Y
100 K

The color range was kept to a minimum. Use was made of the white space of the paper. Text was added in black with black-and-white photographic images highlighted with one or two spot colors such as red and blue.

FONTS

Haettenschweiler
AaBbCcDdEeFfGgHhIiJjKkLlM

Trade Gothic Bold 2
AaBbCcDdEeFfGgHh

Berthold Akzidenz Grotesque
AaBbCcDdEeFfGg

Compacta Bold
AaBbCcDdEeFfGgHhIiJjKk

Eurostile Bold Condensed
AaBbCcDdEeFfGgHhIiJ

Predating the classic Swiss sans-serif faces Helvetica and Univers by two decades, Max Bill's typefaces were clean and unfussy, and often condensed or compressed. The style can be recreated using similar modern fonts.

1

2

3

4

◀ Bill treated black-and-white photographs in a number of different ways using spot color. Add a new layer filled with color beneath the image layer, and change the layer blending mode of the image to **Multiply** (2,3). Alter the color of the image by first changing the **Mode** to **Grayscale**, then applying **Duotone** > **Monotone**, selecting a single color. Change the **Mode** back to CMYK and add a new color-filled background layer (4). Experiment with different blending modes.

▼ ◀ To construct an art concrete-style design, use a grid guide on a division of squares, such as the Illustrator baseboard grid. The final design will be rotated by 45°, so before cropping and coloring the images, rotate each image by -45°. Once color has been added, scale and position the images on the grid, mixing size and color to build the design. Add each image to a new layer to make the construction more flexible.

▼ Once you are satisfied with the arrangement, select all the layers and rotate them 45°. Make any final alterations, if necessary, and add text.

open plan living in the heart of the city

1 coin street

viewing now

1950 > 1959

In the early fifties, because of the devastation of the Second World War, large areas of London were in need of redevelopment. In a bid to boost morale and promote better design, it was decided to hold a national exhibition. Described as "a tonic for the nation," the Festival of Britain, which took place in May 1951, was largely located around London's South Bank, although there were other events held around the country. The festival's official graphic designer was Abram Games, whose innovative combinations of text and image set him apart from his contemporaries. An official war poster artist during the Second World War, Games designed more than one hundred posters during wartime before going on to create the BBC symbol and the identity for the Festival of Britain.

Largely thanks to Alexey Brodovitch's work for *Harper's Bazaar*—and the subsequent design classes he taught both at his home and at New York's New School for Social Research, graphic design in the U.S. was undergoing a revolution. As Otto Storch, one of Brodovitch's students, wrote: "Brodovitch would dump Photostats, type proofs, colored pieces of paper, and someone's shoelace, if it became untied, on a long table together with rubber cement. He would fold his arms and with a sad expression challenge us to do something brilliant." A firm believer that his students should search within each problem for the best solution and execution, Brodovitch was hugely influential not only on the students he taught but also on their eventual approach to design—and resulting work. In the early fifties, Brodovitch also designed the visual arts magazine *Portfolio*, providing the magazine with an elegance and flow that it hadn't previously enjoyed.

By 1954, as the first issue of Hugh Hefner's *Playboy* hit the shelves, and Saul Bass designed his first movie title sequence, the Soviets were focusing on a launch of a different kind: Sputnik. This was also the year that Seymour Chwast, Milton Glaser, and Edward Sorel joined forces to launch the Push Pin Studio. Push Pin Style was the name given to much of the studio's subsequent output, which was more of a pop culture–informed attitude toward visual communication than a particular visual style. Always open to experimentation and new ideas, the studio grew in prominence. Additional designers and illustrators were brought on board and their contributions helped push the boundaries even further.

In the mid-1950s, Saul Bass came into his own as one of the best creators of movie title sequences in the world when he created the titles for Otto Preminger's 1955 film, *The Man With the Golden Arm*. "My initial thoughts about what a title can do was to set mood and the prime underlying core of the film's story, to express the story in some metaphorical way," he said of his work. "I saw the title as a way of conditioning the audience, so that when the film actually began, viewers would already have an emotional resonance with it."

By the end of the decade, the Swiss Style had also really begun to take hold Two of its best-known typefaces, Max Miedinger's Helvetica and Adrian Frutiger's Univers, were designed during this period. And the 1958 launch of *New Graphic Design (Neue Grafik)*, a magazine devoted entirely to the design and typography advocated by the Swiss Style, confirmed its place in the pantheon of graphic design styles.

▲ *Advertisement, Rose Marie Reid, 1958*

MID-CENTURY MODERN

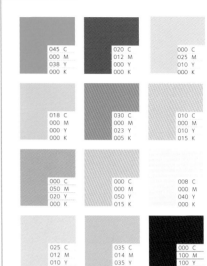

045 C / 000 M / 038 Y / 000 K	020 C / 012 M / 000 Y / 000 K	000 C / 025 M / 010 Y / 000 K
018 C / 000 M / 000 Y / 000 K	030 C / 000 M / 023 Y / 005 K	010 C / 000 M / 010 Y / 015 K
000 C / 050 M / 020 Y / 000 K	000 C / 000 M / 050 Y / 015 K	008 C / 000 M / 040 Y / 000 K
025 C / 012 M / 010 Y / 000 K	035 C / 014 M / 035 Y / 000 K	000 C / 100 M / 100 Y / 030 K

Pastel colors and tints almost define the decade. They were to be found everywhere—in fabrics, wallpapers, furnishings, kitchen equipment, and automobiles. Magazines were no exception.

FONTS

Compacta Light
AaBbCcDdEeFfGgHhIiJjKkLlMmNnOo

Bodoni Poster Compressed
AaBbCcDdEeFfGgHhIiJjKkLlM

Curlz MT Regular
AaBbCcDdEeFfGgHhIi

Bordeaux Roman Bold
AaBbCcDdEeFfGgHhIiJjKkLlMmNnOoPpQ

Fifties typographic design drew on two contrasting influences. One was the Modernist approach developed in Central Europe between the wars and in Switzerland in the 1950s. It produced clean sans-serif letterforms stripped of unnecessary decorative detailing. The other was the use of highly decorative serif fonts with swirling, almost calligraphic detailing. Any of the fonts shown here could usefully be employed to create a fifties "look."

The fifties was a revolutionary era in magazine design, largely due to the work of Alexey Brodovitch. As art director at *Harper's Bazaar* from 1934 to 1958, and through his teaching, Brodovitch was crucial to the introduction of the simplified "modern" graphic style to the U.S. By the fifties, "white space" was the hallmark of Brodovitch's style. The epitome of the modern art director, Brodovitch did not just arrange photographs and type on a page, he played an active role in the conception and commissioning process, often discovering and showcasing young, unknown talent along the way. Another important designer at this time was Cipe Pineles, who, as art director of *Glamour*, became the first autonomous female art director of a mass-market American publication.

▲ Women's Home Companion, *Harry Anderson, 1949*

Title typefaces were often lively and didn't align perfectly on the baseline. The tinted photographs are classic fifties style, and are easy to recreate digitally. Because of the flat tinting, spot colors elsewhere on the page, such as the musical notes, can tie in perfectly with the photograph. The colors also serve to frame text, such as the quote in the corner, and the word "Dress" in the title.

An interesting and playful use of type is typical of the style. This is demonstrated by the highly decorative headline font, the line of type running vertically down the left-hand margin of the page, the text set on a curve above the wagon itself, and the use of spot color to pick out the red of the wagon in both word and image. Magazine "body text" was commonly set as justified left and right.

A wash of pale pink behind these pencil drawings softens what might otherwise have been an overly stark page.

Decorative borders were used to add color and focus. They were usually light, frolicsome motifs.

MID-CENTURY MODERN

◀ Photographs were generally cropped, retouched if necessary, then squared-up and simply positioned on the page for maximum impact. Technological constraints meant that complex cutouts and graphic effects could be time-consuming and expensive. Asked whether he could lay down any rules for picture layout, Brodovitch replied, "There is no recipe for good layout. What must be maintained is a feeling of change and contrast. A layout man should be simple with good photographs. He should perform acrobatics when the pictures are bad."

▲ Typical spread layouts from a weekly women's magazine. The size and position of the images varied across the page. The rules were broken when it came to designing by the grid.

▲ Due to the printing processes and paper quality of the consumer magazines, color reproduction was not true. It sometimes had a hand-tinted quality, or appeared desaturated. Experiment with the **Hue/Saturation** controls, or use one of the preset **Photo Filters** to add red or yellow tones to achieve the look.

▼ Cipe Pineles introduced a very personal style into the art direction of the period. Her fashion spreads at Charm *magazine* were aimed at the new working woman. She often incorporated references to the workspace, wildly out of scale to the model. This is a contemporary take on the style, but it has been given a fifties feel by adjusting the colors. Ladies' fashion was dominated by hats, gloves, and lipstick. The model's lips have been selected and the red saturation increased, and the skin color given a slightly unnatural tone. The color saturation has also been reduced on the background images. Bodoni was one of the favorite font families, especially italicized or compressed.

MID-CENTURY MODERN

At a time when spirits were low and parts of Britain lay in ruins, the Festival of Britain came as a welcome respite. Opened by King George VI on May 3, 1951, this nationwide program of events and exhibitions was organized to mark the centennial of the Great Exhibition of 1851. The festival was also intended to showcase Britain's contribution to civilization in the arts, science, and technology, and in industrial design. The designer responsible for creating the festival's identity was Abram Games. During the Second World War, Games designed numerous posters for the War Office, which appointed him as its official poster artist. Games believed that images should communicate "maximum meaning with minimum means," and his graphic style echoed this. His logo design for the Festival of Britain in 1951 remains his best-known piece of work.

COLOR

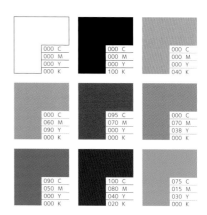

Abram Games mixed strong, brightly colored backgrounds with geometric forms picked out in black and white. For the Festival of Britain, he added spot highlight colors relating to the red, white, and blue of the national flag.

FONTS

Thorne Shaded

ABCDEFGH
1234567890

Festival Titling

ABCDEFGHIJKLMNOPQRS
TUVWXYZ1234567890!?&

Goudy Handtooled

AaBbCcDdEeFfGgH
hIiJjKkLlMmNnOoP

The typical titling fonts were decorative, drop-shadow or two-tone. These were mixed with traditional antique-looking serifs for the secondary information.

▲ *Leaflet*, Festival of Britain, *Abram Games, 1951*

▲ Create a typical background using one of the preset Photoshop textures. A tonal gradient can then be applied either as a layer mask, or on a new layer using a **Transparent to Background** option.

▲ The ball is a simple circle, with finger holes, shadow, and reflection detail added to create the three-dimensional effect. The highlight is created by a simple group of rectangles with a **Warp** > **Arch** distortion applied.

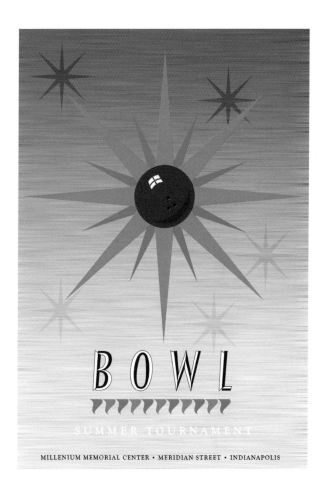

▲ Geometric shapes, usually in the form of stars or diamonds, can be quickly drawn in either Photoshop or Illustrator, using the **Custom Shape** tools. The number of points of a star, and both inner and outer radii, can be specified.

▲ Add color to the stars and vary their scale before combining them to create a "starburst." Use the **Rotate** tool and the **Align** commands.

▲ Arrange each element on a separate layer. Transparency can be adjusted to make the smaller stars recede into the background. Add the text and apply color to emphasize the two-tone effect.

◀ Flags were a common detail of the Festival of Britain designs. Draw a triangular shape and apply a **Warp > Flag** distortion effect. Duplicate, and add alternate colors to complete the "bunting."

MID-CENTURY MODERN

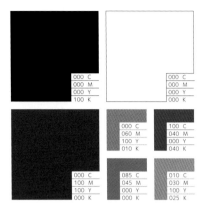

000 C	000 C
000 M	000 M
000 Y	000 Y
100 K	000 K

	000 C	100 C
	060 M	040 M
	100 Y	000 Y
	010 K	040 K

	085 C	010 C
	045 M	030 M
	000 Y	100 Y
	000 K	025 K

000 C	
100 M	
100 Y	
000 K	

Black and white were always featured strongly. Color interest was introduced for backgrounds as an overall, or in the form of panels, but was usually restricted to one or two different hues. Sometimes Bass used a strong blue, bright red, or orange as the dominant background.

FONTS

Vertigo

ABCDEFGHIJKLMN
OPQRSTUVWXYZ

JI Dreary

ABCDEFGHIJKLMN
OPQRSTUVWXYZ

JI Pinder

ABCDEFGHIJKL
MNOPQRSTUVWX

Yahoo

ABCDEFGHI
JKLMNOPQ

Use fonts that look hand-drawn, or resemble letters crudely cut from paper.

The fifties saw the advent of an entirely new film genre thanks to the work of Saul Bass, whose title sequences totally revolutionized the art of film promotion. Prior to this, movie titles were such a non-event that many film projectionists would only pull back the curtains once the title sequence had finished and the film was about to begin. Having already commissioned Bass to design the promotional poster for his 1955 film *The Man With the Golden Arm*, Otto Preminger was so impressed with the results that he asked Bass to create a moving title sequence for the film that incorporated his strong graphics, as well as a soundtrack. And so the medium of animated graphics was born. In subsequent years, Bass collaborated with everyone from Alfred Hitchcock and Stanley Kubrick to Martin Scorsese.

▲ *Movie poster,* The Man With the Golden Arm, *Saul Bass, 1955*

▼ Bass mixed photography with a crude "cutout" style of simplistic illustration. Use the **Pen** tool in a vector application to draw stylized shapes. Drawing skill is not necessary, but use a photograph as a guide if you are unsure. Click points around an object making sharp corners and acute angles. Once you are satisfied with the shape, fill with black.

▼ Create panels of color in the same way. Draw rectangular shapes by quickly clicking several points along the lines to give the impression the shape has been cut from paper. There is no need for accuracy; once the basic shape is drawn, you can stretch or squeeze it to fit the desired space.

▼ Arrange all the elements on the page. Place the photographic images inside black-filled panels, removing any unnecessary background to give a powerful, stark quality. Include one or two colored panels to add interest. Add text, either inside one of the panels, or running round the illustration. Use a font that looks hand-drawn, and vary the size and alignment of the individual letters.

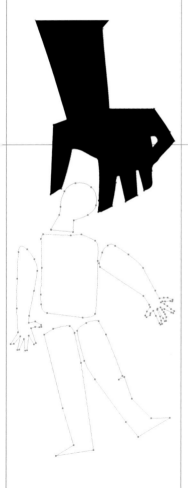

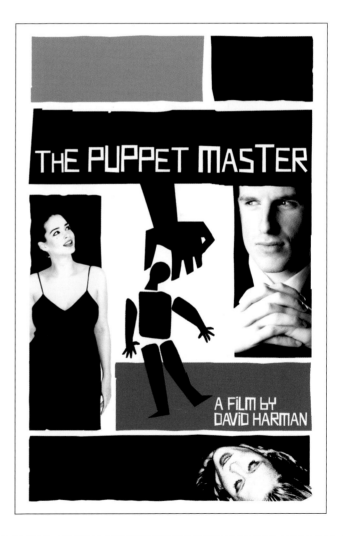

▲ Choose appropriate photographs, convert to **Grayscale**, and increase the **Brightness/Contrast** to make the blacks more pronounced. You can also apply some noise or a **Film Grain** filter to emphasize the grain and give a more "filmic" quality.

MID-CENTURY MODERN

COLOR

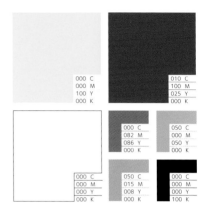

Pastel colors were often used in commercial advertising, though for more eye-catching effect they were accompanied by stronger tones. Candy-floss pink and cream gave way to magenta and strong yellow. Black was kept to a minimum, provided by monochrome photography or illustrative outlines.

The period was one of optimism for most. The U.S. economy had begun to rise for the first time in decades, while, in the U.K., this was the decade that wartime rationing finally came to an end. These changes, coupled with further technological advances, had a noticeable effect on the graphics of the time, particularly in advertising. Until the 1950s, photography had taken a back seat in advertising, largely because illustrations could be produced in color and were also more adaptable. But it wasn't long before the technology had progressed and photography took over as the most vibrant and versatile medium. Photography provided the potential to produce hundreds of possible images from countless angles, instead of just one illustration, making it both the cheaper and faster alternative.

FONTS

Radio AM
AaBbCcDdEeFfGg

Party
AaBbCcDdEeFfGgHhIi

Pepita MT
AaBbCcDdEeFfGg

Park Avenue
AaBbCcDdEeFfGgHhIiJj

Linoscript
AaBbCcDdEeFfGgHhIiJj

Ablefont
ABCDEFGHIJKL

Decorative scripts and typefaces that resembled handwriting introduced a more personal, friendly tone to fifties advertising. These fonts reflected the looser, more abstract styles of illustration.

▲ *Advertisement for Steltomeier & Thiesmann, Sigrid and Hans Lämle, c.1955*

▲ Fashion advertising often employed a looser, sketchier style of illustration. Clip-art libraries stock masses of fashion-related figurative illustration, though it usually looks too contemporary. You can always adapt a figure by combining several originals.

STEP 1 Create the background pattern, or simply use a flat pastel color. Select a suitable model pose (removing it from any background) and place it on a new layer. Now loosely erase areas of the background color with a large brush to create a wash effect.

▲ Small areas of color wash, or pattern, were often used to accentuate the shapes of figures. Gingham and Houndstooth were popular, and can be created by drawing equidistant lines, duplicating, and rotating at 90°.

STEP 2 Select the black outline of the illustration and either copy and paste it into a new layer, or select **Inverse** and delete any color. Adjust the **Brightness/Contrast**, or reduce the layer opacity to make the lines pale gray. As this model's head looks too modern, we will perform some surgery.

STEP 3 A head with a looser drawing style has been selected and added to a new layer, to ease positioning. The longer neck required adjustment, but not much, because this style often accentuated neck length. The black lines of the hair have been selected and copied to another layer. This allows the layer opacity of the head to be reduced so the face outlines are again gray and the face and hair become pale washes. Only the lips remain bright, acting as a focal point. More color has been loosely added to areas of the garment. The all-important fifties accessories, the gloves, have been painted over the hands. Finally, text is added in a hand-written font style.

LATE MODERN

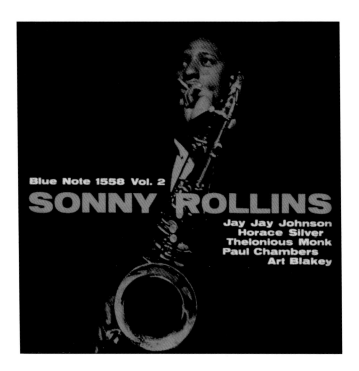

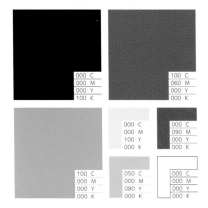

Black, white, and various shades of blue were the signature colors, with the added highlight of a spot color, either on text or as a background tint for a monochrome picture.

In 1939 in mid-Manhattan New York, not far from 52nd Street—where, for a short time, there was more creative jazz per square yard than anywhere else—Blue Note Records was born. The label that came to symbolize the essence of recorded jazz was founded by two German immigrants, Alfred Lion and Francis Wolff. This record company started out in an appropriately improvisational way—symptomatically, the color of the label on the early 78s was the result of a printing error. Nevertheless, the album covers became design icons for the then- new LP vinyl format. The in-house designer was Reid Miles, who for fifteen years created covers in a style that became synonymous with modern jazz. Many of the memorable, even timeless, album photos were taken by Francis Wolff.

The cool graphic style of Blue Note set the standard for album cover design and is often mimicked today, not only by the music industry, but by designers of magazines and book jackets.

FONTS

Compacta Light
AaBbCcDdEeFfGgHhIiJjKkLlMmNnOo

Helvetica Extra Compressed
AaBbCcBbEeFfGgHhIiJjKkLlMm

Helvetica Light Condensed
AaBbCcDdEeFfGgHhIiJjK

Trade Gothic Extended
AaBbCcDdEeF

Bodoni Poster Italic
AaBbCcDdEeFf

Condensed or compressed sans-serif faces, based on the early "Gothic" designs, were typical of the Blue Note style, mixed with extended versions of the same styles. Emphasis was created by scale and color. Occasionally, an ornate serif, even italicized, face was used as an antidote to the cool, clean letterforms.

▲ *LP record sleeve, Harold Feinstein, Photo: Francis Wolff, Blue Note Records, 1957*

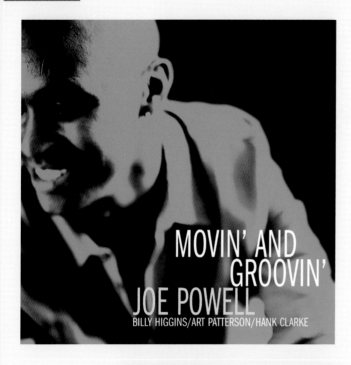

MOVIN' AND
GROOVIN'
JOE POWELL
BILLY HIGGINS/ART PATTERSON/HANK CLARKE

▶ An image with a shallow depth of field, resulting in a receding, blurred background, has been closely cropped for a more dynamic effect.

▼ ▼ ◀ Desaturate the color, or change the color mode to grayscale. Decrease the **Brightness** and increase the **Contrast** to help with "aging." Create a cool mood by making the blending mode **Darken** over a solid blue background.

▲ Black and blue were the dominant colors in the early years. A black-and-white image with the layer blending mode set to **Color Burn** over a blue background will produce the required effect. Stronger, warmer colors were introduced to set moods—"hot" jazz might be inferred by the use of red or magenta.

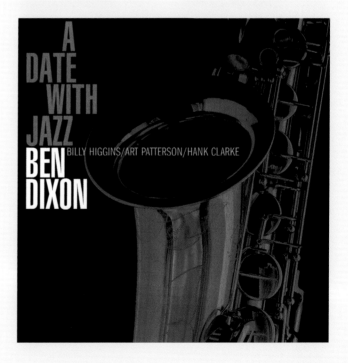

A
DATE
WITH
JAZZ
BEN
DIXON
BILLY HIGGINS/ART PATTERSON/HANK CLARKE

1960 > 1969

Design in the sixties was no longer just about form and function—it was about Style. It was a time of social emancipation; a decade of freedom, of permissiveness, and, most importantly, progress. Moreover, as the postwar baby boomers became teenagers and young adults, this was the decade when the younger generation took control. As the move away from the conservative fifties continued apace, young people were no longer content to grow up as carbon copies of their parents. They wanted change. As youth culture took over as the predominant force, London, Paris, and New York fast became the cultural capitals of a newfound and much celebrated subculture, while further progressions in mass communication paved the way for its development on a truly global scale. All of this was reflected in the designs of the decade. "Design" was now a truly international phenomenon, promoted in part by the lifestyle journals that emerged during the sixties. As youth culture fought against the traditional in favor of fun and irreverence, a number of design styles began to emerge that reflected this buoyant mood.

A young John F. Kennedy spoke of landing on the moon in his famous speech of May 25, 1961, fueling the imaginations of designers and consumers alike. Suddenly, everything from film to fonts to furniture had a futuristic feel. From the space-age graphics of its title sequence to the futuristic forms of the sets, Stanley Kubrick's seminal sci-fi classic *2001: A Space Odyssey* summed up the spirit of the time perfectly.

The anti-establishment beliefs and hippie sentiments of the psychedelic era of the sixties and early seventies had similarities to those of the late nineteenth and early twentieth centuries—both were at first seen as overly radical and found no favor within mainstream culture. Just as Art Nouveau had used the organic shapes and forms inspired by the Arts and Crafts movement as a source of inspiration, so too, did the Psychedelic movement. The Psychedelic aesthetic finally manifested itself in all aspects of cultural production, ranging from art, music, and film to architecture, graphic design, and fashion.

Pop Art was inspired by mass consumerism and popular culture. Its roots can be traced back to the late fifties, but it wasn't until the following decade that it achieved the status of a design style. The very antithesis of all that had gone before, Pop Art rejected not only the idea of Modernism but also the values it represented, openly questioning the precepts of good design. With its bold forms and bright colors, the Pop Art aesthetic was epitomized by the likes of Roy Lichtenstein and Andy Warhol.

By the mid-sixties, a more abstract style of art and graphics, known as Op Art, had begun to emerge, first in Europe and later in the U.S. Short for Optical Art, the style grew from the abstract expressionist movement and used reduced geometric forms to simulate movement. Op Art had a strong influence on both graphic and interior design. Lance Wyman's logo for the 1960 Mexico City Olympic Games epitomized this style.

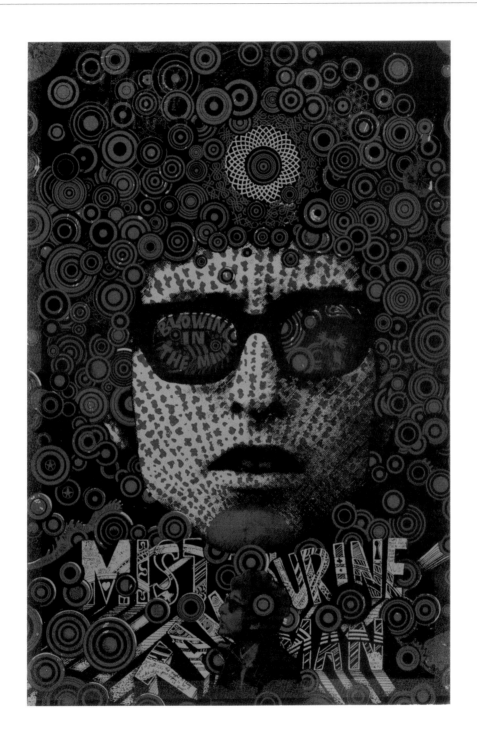

▲ *Poster*, Mr. Tambourine Man, *Martin Sharp, 1964*

POP ART

Richard Hamilton—one of the key exponents of the art form—defined Pop Art as "popular, transient, expendable, low-cost, mass-produced, young, witty, sexy, gimmicky, glamorous, and Big Business." It was a reaction against the clean, sometimes rigid design style of the fifties, and embraced flamboyant populism rather than what its proponents saw as staid elitism.

Pop Art began with Dadaist collages, using cut-up advertisements and everyday graphics to create art. The style quickly expanded to include other forms of consumer-oriented art, such as the photocopied works of Andy Warhol and the large-scale halftone dots of Roy Lichtenstein.

COLOR

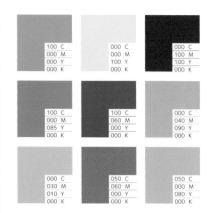

Pop design was inspired by the colors of the rainbow. Vibrant shades were chosen to deliberately create discordant optical effects.

FONTS

Posters and artwork were often hand-lettered, but typography enjoyed its own pop renaissance in the sixties. Fonts such as Revue, Futura Black Extended, Marquee Flash, Capone Light, Rockwell Extra Bold, Dreamland, VAG Rounded Bold, and Revue Drop Shadow (shown above, top to bottom) were typical of the era.

▲ *In the sixties, London was, according to* Time *magazine, "the swinging city," and the Union Jack was adopted as a symbol of the Pop Art movement in the U.K. Its cool credentials were confirmed when it was emblazoned onto a T-shirt worn by Pete Townshend of The Who.*

◄ *Pop Art images were often gloriously bright and flamboyant. Bold colors and dramatic arrangements provided vibrancy, with trails added to objects to suggest movement. The simple lines and shapes gave the feeling that the art could be created by anybody, and wasn't in any way elitist.*

▼ *A halftone dot effect can easily be created from any photograph using Photoshop's* **Sketch** > **Halftone Pattern** *filter. The colors can then be modified using combinations of the* **Image** > **Adjustments** > **Hue/Saturation** *menu, and the* **Stylize** > **Solarize** *filter.*

PSYCHEDELIA

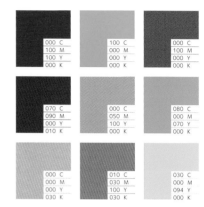

000 C	100 C	000 C
100 M	000 M	100 M
100 Y	000 Y	000 Y
000 K	000 K	000 K

070 C	000 C	080 C
090 M	050 M	000 M
000 Y	100 Y	070 Y
010 K	000 K	000 K

000 C	010 C	030 C
000 M	030 M	000 M
000 Y	100 Y	094 Y
030 K	030 K	000 K

Colors were chosen to invoke the intense visual effects experienced when using mind-altering drugs such as LSD, which were widely adopted by the youth culture of this period. Fluorescent hues were juxtaposed to deliberately clash for the greatest optical vibrancy. Backgrounds were often metallic silver or gold.

FONTS

Butterfield

ABCDEFGHIJKLMNOPQRSTUVWXYZ

Mojo

ABCDEFGHIJKLMNOPQRSTUVWXYZ

Dreamland

abcdefghiJKLMN

Hendrix

ABCDEFGHIJKLMNOP

Playbill

AaBbCcDdEeFfGgHhIiJjKkLlMmNnO

Harking back to Art Nouveau, psychedelic poster fonts were curved and very ornate. The distorted letters were hand-drawn to form curving, swirling lines, or were given multiple radiating outlines. Free-form was the order of the day.

Throughout history the poster has been an important vehicle for the promotion of leisure activities, but the psychedelic rock concerts that characterized the late sixties inspired a particularly raucous style of poster design. It drew inspiration from Art Nouveau's sinuous curves, Op Art's use of optical color vibration, and Pop Art's recycling of images, and was often created by self-taught designers to advertise rock music events and "happenings." The psychedelic experience was translated onto posters and record covers through the use of swirling forms and type and bright colors. The origin of the Psychedelic graphic style is often traced to Wes Wilson. In Britain, Michael English and Nigel Weymouth formed a partnership called Hapshash and the Coloured Coat and produced many psychedelic and surreal posters, record jackets, and murals.

▲ *Poster*, The Soft Machine, *Michael English and Nigel Weymouth, 1967*

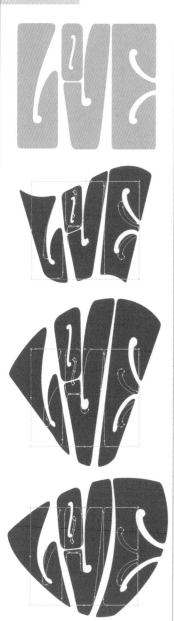

▲ *After distorting the letters, further decoration can be added. This detail from the poster on the opposite page includes spiral motifs. Regular spirals can be created using the Illustrator tool of the same name, then attached to the corners of the distorted type.*

▼ *Butterflies, flowers, targets, sun, moon, and stars interacted with spirals, swirls, and naked women with benign smiling faces—the images of the Peace and Love generation. Using the Illustrator* **Shape** *tools—which include ellipses, stars, and spirals—fantasy illustrations can be created without drawing skills.*

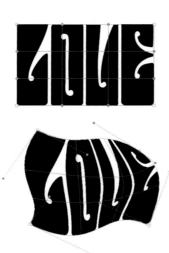

▲ *The Adobe Illustrator* **Edit** > **Warp** *control offers various set distortion options. Increments of horizontal and lateral balance are entered as percentages, so experimentation is required to achieve the desired effect.*

▲ *The Photoshop* **Edit** > **Transform** > **Warp** *command gives more control to the shape of the letters. The number of segments can be preselected, allowing an infinite variation in shape.*

PSYCHEDELIA

Largely a product of California's hippie movement, pop music was the driving force behind the psychedelic explosion of the late 1960s and affected everything from music and art to fashion and design. Psychedelic graphics even found their way into consumer magazines as designers acquired a taste for psychedelia. The self-conscious minimalism and Op Art approach to design was transformed into fantasy-inspired collages of swirling shapes, vivid acid colors, and cartoon-based imagery. While the older generation often found this graphic style virtually illegible, it was perfect for communicating with the youngsters who were able to "decipher rather than read" the message. However, the Psychedelic style was so strong and unsympathetic to other styles that it inevitably departed as quickly as it had arrived, and as early as 1968 was in decline.

METHOD

A vector drawing application such as Illustrator can be used to create radiating psychedelic outlines to a shape or text.

STEP 1 *Type the text, and select a font. Here we have used Vag Rounded, which has a suitable sixties feel. Convert the text to outline. Fill the path with color. Duplicate this layer. Measure the width of one of the ascenders and apply a stroke of twice this value. If the stroke is centered on the path, this will make an outer outline the same width as the letter.*

STEP 2 *Duplicate the outline layer and change the color. Double the stroke width again. As the new layer is hidden below the previous, an outline of the same size is visible.*

STEP 3 *Continue this process, duplicating each layer and alternating the line colors, increasing the stroke width each time, until the page area is completely filled.*

▲ *Poster,* Move at the Marquee, *Michael English, 1967*

STEP 4 *Graduated tints of color merging into each other were a common feature of the style. Open the Illustrator document in Photoshop and make a duplicate layer of the original. Using* **Image** > **Adjustments** > **Hue/Saturation***, manipulate the colors of each layer. Add a layer mask to the top layer, and with the* **Gradient** *tool, draw a vertical line down the center of the mask. This will reveal the layer below, giving a soft, graduated edge. Experiment with the mask by drawing lines of different lengths, until you are satisfied with the result.*

PSYCHEDELIA

The often rather crude line illustrations used by the underground press can be simulated by applying a **Sketch > Photocopy**, or **Stamp** filter to a photographic original. Adjust the light/dark balance to simulate a hand-drawn line.

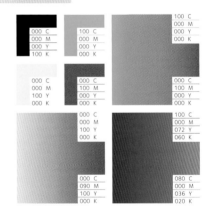

The underground publications were produced on shoestring budgets, often printed on the new web-offset presses. To reduce costs, new methods of adding color to the page were devised. Kaleidoscopic effects were created by printing in multiple or split-fountain hues. Two different color inks were placed in the inkwells at either end of an offset press, so the colors merged when the rollers revolved at high speed, producing additional mixes and blends.

During the sixties, numerous underground magazines and groups sprang up in America and Europe in a wave of idealism promoting alternative communication and democratization. The best known of these was *Oz* magazine, which started in Australia before moving to London in 1966. Its psychedelic graphics and imagery were published under the editorship of Australian Richard Neville. The magazine also featured early writings by the likes of Germaine Greer and Clive James. Much of its psychedelically inspired artwork was created by Martin Sharp, a fellow Australian, best known for his psychedelic rendering of Jimi Hendrix. Other underground titles included the *San Francisco Oracle*, *International Times*, and the *East Village Other*, all of which were testament to the extraordinary burst of creativity and revolution in design and printing techniques that took place during this era.

▲ *OZ magazine cover, Martin Sharp, 1966*

STEP 1 *The split-fountain printing process can be easily simulated using page layout or vector drawing applications. Create a* **New Gradient Swatch** *using the option in the color palette, and simply drag any color to the bar in*

the **Gradient** *tool window. Sliding controls are provided to adjust the size, density, and mix of each color. With Photoshop, color blends can be created by filling new layers with selected color, and applying a* **Layer** *>* **Layer Mask** *>* **Reveal All***.*

STEP 2 *Using the* **Gradient** *tool to click and drag a vertical line over the layer will create a gradient mask, revealing the hidden color of the layer below. Experiment with the position and length of the line and reduce the layer opacity to alter the softness of the blend.*

STEP 3 *Add the illustration to a new layer, removing the background. Reduce the layer opacity a little, to allow some of the background color to show through. Other appropriate imagery can be added, and the blend mode adjusted as required.*

Bad Acid

STEP 4 *Add a headline using a suitable ornate font. Distort the type using* **Edit** *>* **Transform** *>* **Warp***. Select the letters and create a path that can be stroked with color to create an outline. A gradient blend can also be added by duplicating the warped layer and applying a layer mask as before. Body text should be placed in irregular-shaped text boxes, even using ellipses or rounded corners.*

LATE MODERN

Magazine design in the 1960s was dominated by one title—*Twen*. Published from 1959 until 1970, and art-directed by the German Willy Fleckhaus, *Twen* set the style for the decade. Groundbreaking design ideas made full use of the advances in print processes, making *Twen* a leader in magazine layout and design. The magazine's hallmark was the use of solid black pages with type reversed out in white. It was the first publication to print a blue "shiner" ink underneath the process black to give a richness to the page. *Twen* was classy, powerful, and looked intelligent. Many of the titles that emerged in the late sixties and seventies took their design inspiration from *Twen*, including *Nova* and *Avant Garde* magazines.

COLOR

000 C	
000 M	
000 Y	
100 K	

000 C	
090 M	
100 Y	
000 K	

000 C		100 C	
000 M		045 M	
000 Y		000 Y	
000 K		000 K	

Black and white, with the emphasis on black, characterized this Late Modern style. Sometimes spot primary colors were added to text to create typographical impact, but the hallmark of this groundbreaking design was the bold black backgrounds.

FONTS

Helvetica Neue 55 Roman
AaBbCcDdEeFfGg

Helvetica Neue 107 Extra Black Condensed
AaBbCcDdEeFfGgHhli

Helvetica Compressed
AaBbCcDdEeFfGgHhliJjKk

Helvetica Ultra Compressed
AaBbCcDdEeFfGgHhliJjKkLlMmNnO

Helvetica Neue 95 Black Extended
AaBbCcDdEe

Century Expanded
AaBbCcDdEeFfGg

The typographic design of *Twen* was based on the Modernist approach developed in Central Europe between the wars and in Switzerland in the 1950s—clean sans-serif letterforms stripped of unnecessary detail. Headlines were set in condensed or compressed versions and usually all in capitals. Text fonts were mixed: sans serif for the narrow columns and serif for wider, single-column introductory passages, utilizing two or three columns of the grid.

Fleckhaus devised one of the most notable grids ever developed for magazine layout. With this unique 12-unit (also called a 12-lined) grid, he created some superb layouts using varied content. The grid, designed for the large page size of 10½ x 13¼ in (265 x 335 mm), created a single column width of about 4 picas, which was probably never used; but by combining the units, Fleckhaus had the option of working with 6-, 4-, 3-, or 2-column typesetting. The horizontal divisions were coupled with nine divisions of the vertical space, creating a whole series of coordinates for the placement of visual matter and text.

Both text and photographs were often aligned hanging from the top of the page, leaving the foot of the columns deliberately visually ragged. Letter and line spacing were kept tight, creating blocks of text that mimicked the inset pictures. The use of innovative photography was the magazine's trademark. Artfully cropped and often making use of rounded corners, pictures were tightly tied in to the columns of justified text.

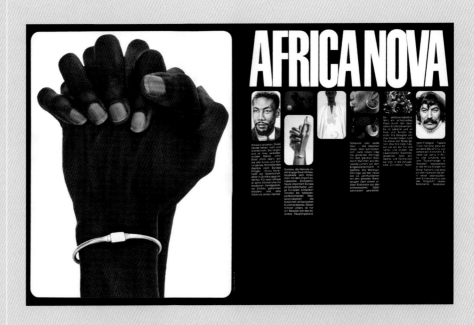

▲ Pages that required large amounts of text never utilized the full grid area, and incorporated headline or "pull-quote"-style text to add visual interest.

▲ White backgrounds made full use of the minimalist "less is more" principle. Headlines were always cleverly aligned with the body copy to create a graphic silhouette.

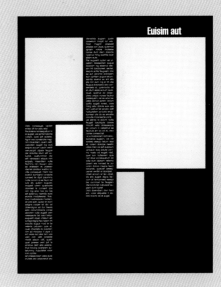

▲ The grid enabled almost limitless creative combinations of text by adjusting the size and format of the images.

147

LATE MODERN

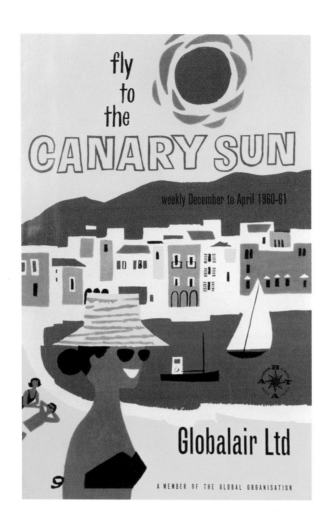

COLOR

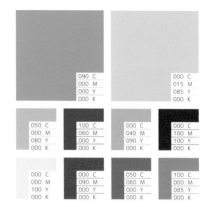

090 C	000 C
000 M	015 M
000 Y	085 Y
000 K	000 K

050 C	100 C	000 C	000 C
000 M	060 M	000 M	100 M
080 Y	000 Y	090 Y	100 Y
000 K	000 K	000 K	000 K

000 C	000 C	050 C	100 C
000 M	090 M	060 M	000 M
100 Y	000 Y	000 Y	085 Y
000 K	000 K	000 K	000 K

The colors of sixties holiday brochures were chosen to evoke the sea, sun, and sand of the vacation destinations. The bright, warm tones were the opposite of the gray drudgery of work, and millions of people were lured in by all that the brochures and posters promised.

FONTS

Marker Felt
AaBbCcDdEeFfGgHhIiJj

Viva
AaBbCcDdEeFfGg

Dax
AaBbCcDdEeFfGgHhIi

Dreary Outline
ABCDEFGHIJKLMN

Title fonts were brash and bold, often with a hand-drawn quality that reflected the casual nature of the product. Fonts were also colored either in similar warm single tones to those used in the imagery, or with two-color gradients or drop shadows to give an eye-catching effect.

The story of mass tourism is one of the most remarkable of the twentieth century, and when package tourism took off in the 1960s and 1970s, few could have imagined the impact it would have. The onset of cheap air travel was accompanied by a host of garish designs created to promote this latest phenomenon. Often illustrated with bright colors, clichéd visual interpretations of life abroad, and quirky "continental" typography, this form of advertising was successful in visually representing the package holiday as something completely new and different.

▲ *Holiday brochure, Globalair Ltd., 1960*

▶ Brochures were full of as many images as possible, so that the eye was immediately drawn to the alluring pictures. The body text—filled with similarly colorful and evocative descriptions of locations—was secondary to the images, and often in a smaller than average point size. Print quality was improving rapidly throughout the decade, and color images were rich and detailed.

▼ The bold colors and lines of package holiday posters can easily be recreated in vector software, such as Adobe Illustrator. The freeform lines are all created using the **Pen** tool, while the geometric shapes are formed with a combination of the **Rectangle** tool and the **Pen** tool constrained to straight lines. The boats have simply been duplicated then scaled and flipped to create variety.

REVIVAL

As the swinging sixties continued apace, many designers found themselves looking back to the twenties and Art Nouveau for inspiration. Set up by Milton Glaser, Seymour Chwast, Reynold Ruffins, and Edward Sorel in 1954, Push Pin Studios had a major impact on the visual design of the 1960s and 1970s and represented an important chapter in postwar graphic design. The Push Pin partners began by producing a publication—the *Push Pin Almanack* (later the *Push Pin Graphic*)—to promote their services. Primarily illustrators, Push Pin were keen to offer an alternative to the photography that dominated modern graphic design at the time. Their flowing ink lines and use of techniques such as woodcut, collage, and painting on wood (which the studio pioneered) were hugely influential and successful both in the U.S. and around the world.

COLOR

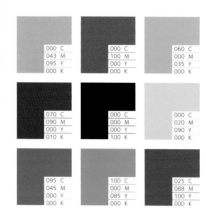

000 C	000 C	060 C
043 M	100 M	000 M
095 Y	000 Y	035 Y
000 K	000 K	000 K

070 C	000 C	000 C
090 M	000 M	020 M
000 Y	000 Y	090 Y
010 K	100 K	000 K

095 C	100 C	025 C
045 M	000 M	088 M
000 Y	085 Y	100 Y
000 K	000 K	000 K

Push Pin graphic design was led by illustration, incorporating a wide color spectrum, and it is difficult to isolate a particular palette. Milton Glaser's illustration often mixed the bright colors of the era, though he claims, "Most designers use primaries at full intensity. I always try to get more into tonality and nuance, which is much more playful."

FONTS

Rainbow
AABBCCDDEEFFGGHHI

Baby Teeth
ABCDEFGHIJKLM

Buffalo
ABCDEFGHIJK

Monograph
ABCDEFGHIJKLM

Baby Fat
ABCDEFABCDEF

During the 1960s, both Seymour Chwast and Milton Glaser designed several display typefaces. Many were inspired by vintage Victorian, Art Deco, Art Nouveau, and Italian Futurist originals.

   ▲ *Columbia Records poster, Dylan, Milton Glaser, 1966*

STEP 1 *Milton Glaser's image of Bob Dylan is a seminal piece of 1960s design. The simplicity of the stark profile combined with psychedelic hair was a masterstroke. To emulate this classic, choose a profile with well-defined features, preferably set against a neutral background.*

STEP 2 *Use* **Image** > **Adjustments** > **Threshold** *to convert the photographic original into a silhouette. Any areas of the profile not converted to solid black can be filled by hand with a hard brush.*

STEP 3 *Using a vector drawing application, create a series of concentric circles with a white background and black stroke. Group the shapes and copy and paste them into a new layer in Photoshop. Duplicate the layer several times and randomly scale each. Simply apply color as required, using the* **Magic Wand** *and* **Eyedropper** *tools.*

STEP 4 *Draw freehand shapes and swirls with a* **Pen** *tool. Keep a black outline stroke and a white fill, and ensure each new shape is on a new layer. The shapes can be duplicated and repositioned or distorted, and color can be added as in the previous step. Create a balance by leaving some areas white.*

STEP 5 *Continue to add shape and color, repositioning as you go, until a satisfactory result is achieved. Fill the background behind the hair with black to intensify the effect of the color. Add a minimal amount of text. Glaser's Baby Teeth, the font used in the Dylan poster, is very similar to Constructivist Block, by P22 type foundry.*

1970 > 1989

The American graphic designer and photographer Herb Lubalin was a prominent force during the seventies. In addition to his considerable skill as a typeface designer, Lubalin had become increasingly aware of the ease with which original type designs could now be copied. Determined to ensure that the designers who had spent so many hours laboring over their work were adequately compensated, Lubalin teamed up with Edward Rondthaler and Aaron Burns to found the International Typeface Corporation (ITC) to develop and license typefaces. ITC fonts followed the example set by Univers and Helvetica, which, with their large x-heights and short ascenders and descenders, were characteristic of many fonts designed during the seventies and early eighties.

In advertising, 1971 was the year that the now infamous Nike swoosh was designed—not, as one might think, by a hotshot designer but by a student, Carol Davidson. The logo was bought by Nike for just $35. Three years on, Milton Glaser said goodbye to Push Pin Studio to found Milton Glaser Inc. A year later he would create one of America's most well-known—and loved—graphic devices, I♥NY. Elsewhere, CBS Records had consolidated its reputation for creating some of the most innovative album covers around, thanks to designers such as Paula Scher.

As NASA launched its first-ever space shuttle in 1977, the emergence of Punk in the U.K. was having a huge influence on contemporary culture. Affecting everything from music and art to fashion and literature, the London Punk scene was epitomized by the Sex Pistols. With its cut 'n' paste-style graphics and straight-to-the-point messages, the Punk art that graced the album covers of the time was often highly political. Some of the best known of these are Jamie Reid's covers for the Sex Pistols' *Never Mind the Bollocks Here's the Sex Pistols* album and "God Save the Queen" single.

From a design perspective, the eighties got off to a fantastic start with the launch of Terry Jones's *i-D* magazine in London. With its spontaneous graphics, what started out as a street-style fanzine would go on to become one of the most influential style bibles of its time. The following year, Neville Brody's appointment as art director of *The Face* had a similar impact, not only on fashion and magazine culture but also on the world of advertising.

For much of the twentieth century, graphic design had been a time-consuming and laborious process. Designs could not be visualized unless they were laid out by hand. Experimenting with different fonts at the click of a mouse simply wasn't an option, as all type had to be ordered from typesetters. However, as technology continued to advance and new computer software became available, the graphic design process was revolutionized. The arrival of computers meant there was no longer any need for a separate typesetter as designers now had the tools to do the job themselves. The novelty of this progression led to many younger designers taking an experimental approach to editorial design. Advances in software, too, equipped designers with the ability to do everything from stretching and layering type to creating the most complex montages. Early pioneers of this new technology included Los Angeles–based designer April Greiman, whose digital collages and use of layered digitized imagery soon became her calling card, and Rudy VanderLans, whose magazine *Émigré* launched in 1984.

▲ The Face *magazine cover, Neville Brody, 1985*

LATE MODERN

COLOR

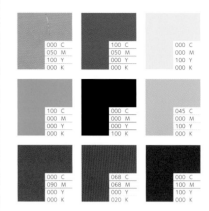

000 C 050 M 100 Y 000 K	100 C 050 M 000 Y 000 K	000 C 000 M 100 Y 000 K
100 C 000 M 000 Y 000 K	000 C 000 M 000 Y 100 K	045 C 000 M 100 Y 000 K
000 C 090 M 000 Y 000 K	068 C 068 M 000 Y 020 K	000 C 100 M 100 Y 000 K

The Cuban poster artists borrowed ideas from Pop Art and psychedelia as well as the ethnic roots of local folklore. The red of the communist star mixed with bright Hispanic-influenced hues. The revolutionary struggle was often portrayed using the vibrant colors associated with Latin dance.

FONTS

Typographic information was brief and to the point. Bold sans-serif roman and condensed faces acted more as captions to the image than headlines. Naive, hand-drawn lettering and decoration featured bright colors and multiple outlines so the political messages would be understood by the uneducated masses.

From the 1960s to the 1980s, posters were used in Cuba to promote everything from the country's huge sugar harvests and national literacy campaigns, to film and music, to its opposition to the U.S. war in Vietnam. Rather than any specific aesthetic design cues, Cuban poster art was characterized by its wide-ranging content and style. Moreover, Cuba was small enough that posters were regarded as a perfectly viable medium for reaching wide audiences, and, although the worlds of "fine art" and "commercial art" continued to exist, many artists found they could make a perfectly adequate living by using their design skills to promote services and help build communities. International solidarity was also an important part of Cuban culture, and as a result, many of the posters designed during this period highlighted Cuban resistance to U.S. imperialism.

STEP 1 *A graphic trick of the Cuban poster artist was the repetition of a single image to reinforce a message. This poster promoting the U.S. Fire Department started life as a four-color image. A portrait of a firefighter has been converted to black-and-white lines using the* **Stamp** *filter, then the black and white areas selected with the* **Magic Wand***, and filled with a chosen color.*

STEP 2 *Duplicate the layer several times, and* **Edit** > **Transform** > **Scale** *to enlarge each new layer as you go, to build a tiled image. A different layer blend mode has been applied to each layer. Try modes such as* **Multiply**, **Hard Mix**, **Difference***, and* **Color Dodge***.*

STEP 4 *Don't worry if changing the blend modes does not produce a pleasing result. Once the image is flattened, it is easy to select certain areas of color with the* **Magic Wand** *tool and add any new color you want. The overall hues can also be modified using* **Hue/Saturation***.*

Text played a secondary role in the Cuban style, so keep the text to a minimum, and use small font sizes.

STEP 3 *Color has been applied to an image of a map of the U.S. This is copied into a new layer in the master document, and duplicated two or three times. The map layers are placed at intervals separating the portrait layers. A different layer blend mode was then applied to each map layer. The portrait layers will again affect the blend mode choices of the separating maps.*

157

LATE MODERN

During the seventies, art directors like Herb Lubalin set the pace, gaining much acclaim for their bold, intricate layouts and typographic experimentation. Described as "the typographic genius of his time," Lubalin focused primarily on space and surface, abandoning the traditional rules of typography and layout in the process. Finding the constraints of metal type too restricting, Lubalin would cut up his type proofs and reassemble them, enabling him to compress, enlarge, join or even overlap the type as he desired. As a result, words could become images and vice versa; he could make type walk or transform words into typograms. In Lubalin's hands, letters were no longer merely vessels of form, they were objects of meaning. Lubalin was also one of the pioneers of phototypography, a process that involved setting type by exposing negatives of alphabetic characters to photographic paper.

COLOR

100 C	000 C	000 C
050 M	100 M	000 M
000 Y	100 Y	000 Y
000 K	000 K	100 K

▲ Color was used sparingly, to highlight a certain heading or block of type, and restricted to a primary red or blue. Tints of black also created visual emphasis. Lubalin also used bolder typeface weights to add texture and color to a page.

▶ Lubalin's hallmark style of combining large headlines with tightly kerned blocks of text was perfected using phototypography, manipulating the letters using distorting lenses to create exaggerated disparity of scale. Lubalin also often employed oversized punctuation or speech marks. This style is second nature to anyone used to setting type with digital word-processing software. Kerning, tracking, and leading can all be adjusted to the minutest increment using keystrokes.

FONTS

Din Schrift 1451 Engschrift Alternate
AaBbCcDdEeFfGgHhIiJjKkLl

ITC Franklin Gothic
ABCDEFGHIJKLMN

ITC Cheltenham Book
AaBbCcDdEeFfGgH

ITC Stone Serif
AaBbCcDdEeFfGgH

ITC Lubalin Graph
AaBbCcDdEeFfGg

Avant Garde Gothic BT
AÆBCDEFGHIJKLMN

Lubalin designed the *Avant Garde* magazine logo (featured as part of the exclamation mark, left), which was developed into a full typeface by Tom Carnase for commercial distribution in 1970. That same year, Lubalin cofounded the International Typeface Corporation, which over the decade designed 34 type families and 60 display faces.

Graphic Type

The American designer & photographer Herb Lubalin was a prominent force during the seventies

In addition to his considerable skill as a face designer, Lubalin had become increasingly aware of the ease with which original type designs could now be copied. Determined to ensure the designers who spent so many hours labouring over their work were adequately compensated, Lubalin teamed up with Edward Rondthaler & Aaron Burns to found the International Typeface Corporation (ITC) to develop and license typefaces. ITC fonts followed the example set by Univers and Helvetica, which, with their large x-heights and short ascenders and descenders, were characteristic of many fonts designed during the seventies and early eighties.

Style

IN ADVERTISING, 1971 WAS THE YEAR THAT THE NOW INFAMOUS NIKE SWOOSH WAS DESIGNED – NOT, AS ONE MIGHT THINK, BY A HOT SHOT DESIGNER BUT BY A STUDENT, CAROL DAVIDSON.

CBS records had consolidated its reputation for creating some of the most innovative new album covers thanks to designers such as Paula Scher. As nasa launched its first ever space shuttle, the emergence of punk in the UK in 1976, was having a

style

THE LOGO FOR JUST $35. BOUGHT BY NIKE THREE YEARS ON, MILTON GLASER SAID GOODBYE TO PUSH PIN STUDIO TO FOUND MILTON GLASER INC. A YEAR LATER HE WOULD CREATE ONE OF AMERICA'S MOST WELL-KNOWN AND LOVED GRAPHIC DEVICES.

style

huge influence on contemporary culture. affecting everything from music, to art, fashion and literature the London punk scene was epitomised by the Sex Pistols. With its cut 'n' paste style graphics and to-the-point messages.

JAPANESE MODERN

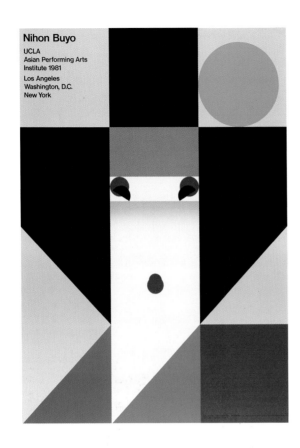

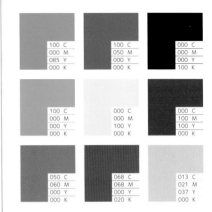

100 C 000 M 085 Y 000 K	100 C 050 M 000 Y 000 K	000 C 000 M 000 Y 100 K
100 C 000 M 000 Y 000 K	000 C 000 M 100 Y 000 K	000 C 100 M 100 Y 000 K
050 C 060 M 000 Y 000 K	068 C 068 M 000 Y 020 K	013 C 021 M 037 Y 000 K

Tanaka used a simple, strong primary palette, with a predominance of black. Red circles mimic the rising sun of the national flag and neutral backgrounds symbolize the Japanese landscape.

Japanese design makes use of four different sets of characters. Pictograms (*Kanji*), phonetic characters (*Katakana*), cursive forms (*Hiragana*), and the Western alphabet. Sometimes different sets and styles are mixed for visual effect.

Graphic design was a relatively new discipline in Japan after the Second World War. Both European Constructivism and Western design were important influences on Japanese graphic designers, resulting in a new design style that incorporated international influences while still retaining its national traditions. A diverse range of iconography, including *manga* comic books, popular sci-fi movies, and, of course, the traditional family crest also provided inspiration. Ikko Tanaka was a key figure in the promotion of modern Japanese graphic design. His work, both creatively and as a founding member of the Nippon Design Center, helped bring a much-needed level of professionalism and focus to this new discipline. Tanaka's designs reworked traditional Japanese themes in modern graphic styles, using abstract motifs and geometric forms.

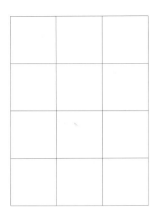

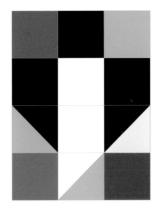

▲ Tanaka's poster was designed to a rigid grid and formed from simple geometric shapes reminiscent of Chinese tangrams. Even though the shapes used are so simple, the image is instantly recognizable as

the traditional Japanese geisha style with kimono, white makeup, and hair worn up. It is easy to create a series of designs based upon this image by altering the color scheme and facial features.

◄ A circular element introduced in the top corner represents the sun. By making the two top-corner pieces the same color, a simple background is created to set the portrait against. The pink graduated tint on the face suggests both geisha makeup and the blushing innocence of the subject.

JAPANESE MODERN

Opening his first design office in 1970, Japanese designer Takenobu Igarashi developed an individual style creating three-dimensional alphabets. He incorporates these "architectural alphabets" into both graphic work and sculpture used for signage. The alphabets are drawn on an isometric grid and are diverse in their complexity. Letters appear to explode into multiple parts, or to be constructed from different materials. They are created using dot, line, surfaces, and basic geometric forms of circle and square, the grids bringing mathematical order to the work.

DESIGN

Isometric-style alphabets can be easily created without the need for sophisticated 3D software, using Illustrator copy and paste commands and the alignment tools. Outline the letters and rotate the word to an angle of 30º. Then copy and paste several times to create a tight stack. Fill and outline the stacked elements and distribute evenly in a vertical axis, aligning them to the left.

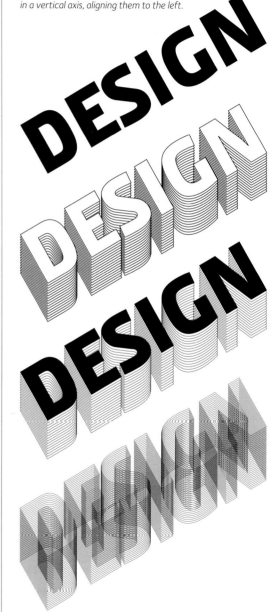

◀ The "stacked" sets of duplicated letters can be graphically treated in all sorts of ways. Add isometric grid lines by copying and duplicating a line drawn with the **Pen** tool. Vary the number of duplicated elements for each individual letter, or alter the alignment. Add color or texture to stacks, varying the color of the topmost element. Group the individual letter stacks and change their order using the **Send to Back** command.

▼ A more genuine isometric 3D form can be created by selecting all the elements in a single stack of letters (except the top element), and applying the **Pathfinder** > **Add to Shape Area** tool, and expanding the shape. The result will be an outline of the shape, but the verticals are formed from zigzags. These can be removed with the **Delete Anchor Point** tool, or simply deleted and replaced with a vertical rule. Color fills, strokes, and textures selected from the **Style** libraries can then be applied.

PUNK

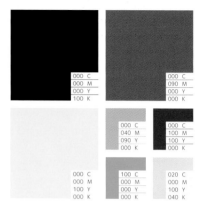

NEVER MIND
THE BOLLOCKS
HERE'S THE
Sex Pistols

Arguably the most influential style of the seventies, Punk remained an underground scene until 1976, when two bands—the Ramones in the U.S. and the Sex Pistols in the U.K.—brought it to the mainstream. With its anti-establishment ethic and DIY approach to everything from fashion to music to design, Punk captured the imagination of an entire generation. The style also had a huge influence on the graphics of the day, as pioneered by Jamie Reid. With his brash, distinctive cut'n'paste style, Reid perfectly captured Punk's DIY ethic with his own style of visual anarchy. His best-known works include the legendary Sex Pistols album *Never Mind the Bollocks Here's the Sex Pistols* and the singles "Anarchy in the U.K.," "God Save the Queen," and "Pretty Vacant."

COLOR

000 C 000 M 000 Y 100 K	000 C 090 M 000 Y 000 K
000 C 040 M 090 Y 000 K	000 C 100 M 100 Y 000 K
000 C 000 M 100 Y 000 K	100 C 000 M 000 Y 000 K / 020 C 000 M 100 Y 040 K

Gritty black and white dominated Punk graphics. Color, introduced as spot and flat background, was strong and bright. Reid used fluorescent colors, difficult to print, for some of his album sleeves, often resulting in impure color variations.

FONTS

aNYthinG GOes

Choose fonts at random, selecting a different font for each letter to simulate a cutout collage.

▲ *Record sleeve,* Never Mind the Bollocks Here's the Sex Pistols, *Jamie Reid, 1977*

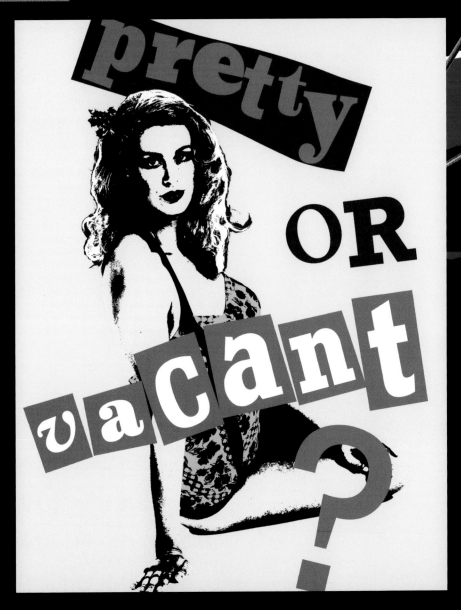

▲ Roughly cut or torn edges are synonymous with the Punk style: either scan a real torn edge or draw an irregular line with the **Pen** tool. Buckles, zippers, and pins were the iconic fashion accessories.

▲ Image quality was disregarded, or rather deliberately distressed. The photocopier was used to remove the subtle gray tones and areas were colored by hand. The effect can be digitally created using the **Stylize** > **Torn Paper** filter and adjusting the contrast control until the desired level of hardness is achieved.

▲ Set the type as individual letters, varying the font, size, and rotation to produce a random arrangement. Draw freehand shapes to sit behind individual letters or words to simulate the cutout collage. Ignore all the rules and guides, just place elements by eye.

▲ Images were often cut from newsprint to reinforce the DIY effect. Apply the **Sketch** > **Halftone Pattern** filter to a digital image to simulate the effect.

COLOR

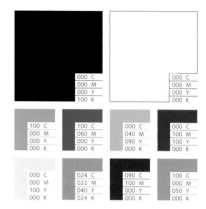

000 C 000 M 000 Y 100 K	000 C 000 M 000 Y 000 K

100 C 000 M 000 Y 000 K	100 C 060 M 000 Y 000 K	000 C 040 M 090 Y 000 K	000 C 100 M 100 Y 000 K
000 C 000 M 100 Y 000 K	024 C 022 M 040 Y 024 K	090 C 100 M 000 Y 000 K	100 C 000 M 050 Y 000 K

The return of white (or black) space was central to the Brody layout. Full-page bleed photography was set alongside bold black typography. Warm gray or strong color bleed backgrounds were also incorporated. The title or a single word of the title might also be injected with color.

The age of computer-based design completely transformed the world of graphics as designers found themselves in complete control, able to blend, stretch, and scale, all at the click of a mouse. One of the first to challenge the conventions of graphic design during this period was British designer, Neville Brody. With the advent of the first Apple Macs, Brody began to set new precedents in design and typography through his experimental and challenging work, first in record-cover design and then as art director of *The Face* magazine from 1981 to 1986. Moving on to *Arena* in 1987, Brody took a step back to focus on minimal, non-decorative typography before later developing this into a more painterly style. In 1988, Brody published the first of his two monographs, *The Graphic Language of Neville Brody*, which quickly became one of the world's best-selling graphic-design books.

FONTS

Helvetica Roman
AaBbCcDdEeFfGgHh

Helvetica Black
AaBbCcDdEeFfGg

Franklin Gothic Book
AaBbCcDdEeFfGgHhIi

Franklin Gothic Extra Condensed
AaBbCcDdEeFfGgHhIiJjKkLlM

Didot
AaBbCcDdEeFfGgH

In the early days of the "style magazine" Brody used "unemotional" sans-serif gothics—Helvetica and Franklin Gothic (Extra Condensed for the titles) in an attempt to "pursue the power of simplicity." He also experimented with more classical faces; Didot was introduced in a redesign of *Lei* magazine. Brody is also renowned for designing his own typefaces.

▲ Arena *magazine cover, Neville Brody, November 1988*

▶ *Brody was commissioned to restructure and redesign Italian Condé Nast publications* Per Lui *and* Lei. *He combined closely cropped photographs with clean, bold typography, creating dynamic shapes by setting both headline and text in disparate sizes on both the horizontal and vertical axes.*

▶ *The design of* Arena *magazine, launched in 1986, was originally intended to be "boring," to focus the readers' attention on the subject matter. Brody soon became "bored with the boredom" and introduced a more expressive, painterly use of the typography. Headlines were tightly kerned and leaded, with lines often overlapping one another. Letters were individually scaled and flowed across the page, often bleeding off the trim or into the gutter.*

REFERENCE

GLOSSARY

ADJUSTMENT LAYER A layer that contains no image pixels but affects the appearance of layers below it in the layer "stack." These include changes to levels, contrast, and color, plus gradients and other effects. These changes do not permanently affect the pixels underneath, so by masking or removing the adjustment layer, you can easily remove the effect from part or all of an image with great ease. You can also change an adjustment layer's parameters at a later point, even after restarting Photoshop.

ALIASING Ragged rendering caused by digitizing subtle forms onto a fixed grid.

ALPHA CHANNEL A channel that stores selections in Photoshop.

ANTIALIASING Shading applied to the jagged edge of a digital character to simulate smoothness.

BACKGROUND LAYER The bottom layer in the Layers palette that cannot be moved, made transparent, or have a blending mode or layer style applied to it. It can be converted into a regular layer.

BASELINE An imaginary line on which the bases of capitals and most lowercase letters rest.

BASELINE GRID A temporary grid of horizontal lines at fixed intervals that can be adjusted as required.

BITMAP A "map" describing the location and binary state (on, off) of bits. It defines a complete collection of pixels that comprise an image, such as a letter.

BLENDING MODE The way in which layers interact and how a layer's pixels and color information affect the underlying layers. This produces a result based on the base color and the blending mode.

BODY TEXT Typesetting forming the main portion of a book or other printed matter.

BOLD FACE A heavier variant of the normal roman of a given typeface.

BRIGHTNESS The relative lightness or darkness of a color, measured as a percentage from 0% (black) up to 100% (white).

CENTERED A typographic arrangement that appears symmetrical on the page.

CHANNELS In Photoshop, a color image is usually composed of three or four separate single-color images, called Channels. In standard RGB mode, the Red, Green, and Blue channels will each contain a monochromatic image representing the parts of the image that contain that color. In a CMYK image, the channels will be Cyan, Magenta, Yellow, and Black. Individual channels can be manipulated in much the same way as the main image.

CMYK Cyan, Magenta, Yellow, and Black. The four printing-process colors based on the subtractive color model (black is represented by the letter K, which stands for "key plate"). In color reproduction, most of the colors are achieved by mixing cyan, magenta, and yellow; the theory being that when all three are combined, they produce black. However, this is rarely achievable—and would be undesirable as too much ink would be used, causing problems with drying time, etc. For this reason, black is used to add density to darker areas—while, to compensate, smaller amounts of the other colors are used (this also has cost benefits, as black is cheaper than colored inks).

CONDENSED A typeface variant that is narrower than the basic roman font.

CONTRAST The degree of difference between adjacent tones in an image, from the lightest to the darkest.

CROP To trim or mask an image so that it fits a given area or so that unwanted portions can be discarded.

DESATURATE A quick way to make a color image black and white by equalizing the Red, Green, and Blue channel values.

DROP CAPITAL A large initial capital letter at the beginning of a paragraph that occupies space on several lines below.

EPS Encapsulated PostScript. A standard graphics file format used primarily for storing vector graphics files generated by "drawing applications" such as Adobe Illustrator and Macromedia FreeHand. An EPS file usually has two parts: one containing the PostScript code that tells the printer how to print the image, the other an onscreen preview, which can be in PICT, TIFF, or JPEG formats.

EXPANDED A typeface variant proportionally wider than the basic roman.

EXPERT SET An additional font of characters, extra to the standard character set. It can include non-aligning figures (OSF), small capitals (SC), fractions, and other signs.

EYEDROPPER A tool used to select the foreground or background color from colors in an image or from a selectable color swatch. Eyedroppers are also used to sample colors in other Photoshop dialogs, including the Levels or Color Range dialogs.

FACE The visual identity of a typeface.

FAMILY The related weights, italics, condensed, and expanded forms of a typeface.

FAT-FACE A 19th-century display type of dramatically heavy weight or thickness.

FEATHER An option used to soften the edge of a selection, in order to hide the seams between adjusted or manipulated elements and neighboring areas.

FIXED WORD-SPACING Word-spacing in a passage of typesetting that is the same unit throughout; when set flush left it creates ragged line endings.

FLUSH LEFT Typesetting in which the lines are aligned on the left.

FONT A complete set of characters, capitals, lower case, figures, and punctuation. In metal typesetting, a font consisted of a quantity of each character in proportion to other letters to fill a typecase.

GLYPH A shape of a character, accent, or symbol, irrespective of its name.

GRADIENT TOOL Allows the creation of a gradual blend between two colors within a selection. Several types exist, including linear, radial, and reflected gradients.

GRAYSCALE A black-and-white image in which pixel brightness values are recorded on a scale of 0 to 255 for black to white.

Unlike RGB or CMYK images, a grayscale image has no color information.

HALFTONE A technique of reproducing a continuous tone image on a printing press by breaking it up into a pattern of equally spaced dots of varying size—the larger the dots, the darker the shade.

HEAVY A variant of a type family, usually darker than bold.

H&J Hyphenation and Justification. The part of the computer program that deals with word breaks and word spacing.

HUE Color expressed as a degree between 0° and 360° on the standard color wheel or normally referred to as red, orange, or green, etc. See Saturation.

HYPHENATION The breaking of words, ideally at the end of a syllable, in order to fit a measure.

IMPRINT The information concerning copyright, printing, and publishing history of a book. Usually found on the reverse side of the title page.

INDENT A common method of identifying a paragraph by leaving a blank space at the start of a line.

ITALIC A companion typeface to roman, with a cursive appearance.

JUSTIFICATION The process of adjusting words and spaces to fit a measure.

KERNING The adjustment of pairs or groups of letters to improve letterfit.

LAYER A feature used to produce composite images by "suspending" image elements on separate "overlays." Once these layers have been created, they can be re-ordered, blended, and have their transparency (opacity) altered.

LEADING Interlinear spacing of lines of type. Originally strips of lead of various thicknesses.

LIGHT A fine-weight variant in a family of typefaces.

MARGINS The white space between the printed area of a page and the trimmed edge. They consist of the head margin, the foot margin, the fore-edge margin, and the spine margin.

MEASURE The width of a column to which a line of type is set.

MONOSPACED An alphabet of letters of a single-unit width throughout.

OPACITY In a layered Photoshop document, the percentage of transparency that each layer of an image has in relation to the layer beneath. As the opacity is lowered, the layer beneath shows through.

OPENTYPE Cross-platform font format allowing TrueType and Type 1 fonts to be enclosed in one "wrapper" and offering the possibility of a large character set.

ORNAMENTS Typographic sorts and borders used for decoration.

OUTLINE A typeface formed as an outline rather than solid strokes.

PEN TOOL A tool used for drawing vector paths in Photoshop and Illustrator.

PHOTOCOMPOSITION The production of typesetting by use of a keyboard for input, and the use of a photo unit to produce output.

PHOTOTYPESETTING The produce of photocomposition; usually a bromide print.

PIXEL Acronym for picture element. The smallest component of a digitally generated image, such as a single dot of light on a computer monitor. In its simplest form, one pixel corresponds to a single bit: 0 = off and 1 = on. In color and grayscale images or monitors, a single pixel may correspond to several bits: an 8-bit pixel, for example, can be displayed in any of 256 colors (the total number of different configurations that can be achieved by eight 0s and 1s).

POINT The basic typographic unit of measurement. It is a term used by both the Anglo-American and the European Didot system.

POSTSCRIPT Adobe's patent page description language; it enables vector-based outlines to be rasterized efficiently.

PPI Pixels per inch. The most common unit of resolution, describing how many pixels are contained within a single square inch of image.

RAGGED Typesetting that is aligned on the left with fixed word-spacing, creating a ragged right alignment.

RASTERIZATION The conversion of outlines into dots.

RESOLUTION The degree of quality, definition, or clarity with which an image is reproduced or displayed on screen or the printed page. The higher the resolution, the more pixels are contained within a given area, and the greater the detail captured.

RGB Red, Green, Blue. The primary colors of the "additive" color model—used in video technology (including computer monitors) and also for graphics (for the Web and multimedia, for example) that will not ultimately be printed by the four-color (CMYK) process method.

RUNAROUND A column of text composition is adjusted to fit around what is generally an irregular-shaped illustration.

SANS-SERIF A letterform that does not have serifs.

SATURATION The strength or purity of a color. Saturation is the percentage of gray in proportion to the hue: 100% is fully saturated. On the standard color wheel, saturation increases from the center to the edge. Also called chroma.

SERIF The short finishing stroke projecting from the end of a letter's stem. These consist of several varieties of form, and give the typeface its particular character.

SLAB-SERIF An early 19th-century typeform, with serifs of similar thickness to the stems; also called Egyptian.

SMALL CAPS An alphabet of capital letters that align with the x-height of a font.

UNICODE An international standard digital code for describing a character set.

UNJUSTIFIED A typeset column that is aligned flush on the left and ragged on the right.

VECTOR GRAPHICS A graphics file that uses mathematical descriptions of lines, curves, and angles. When using vector graphics, it does not matter how large or small you print the file; it will still reproduce perfectly because there are no bitmapped pixels.

WEIGHT The overall line thickness of a typeface, which creates the color on the page.

INDEX

INDEX

ACKNOWLEDGMENTS

Picture Acknowledgments

13: Robert Opie Collection; 15: Library of Congress, Washington, DC; 16, 18: Robert Opie Collection; 24: Corbis/Swim Ink 2, LLC; 28: Hunterian Museum and Art Gallery, University of Glasgow; 30: Österreichische Nationalbibliothek, Wien; 40: University College London, Special Collections; 43: Robert Opie Collection; 44: © El Lissitzky. Licensed by DACS 2006; 46: Courtesy The Rodchenko Archive © Alexander Mikhailovich Rodchenko. Licensed by DACS 2006; 48: Corbis/Swim Ink 2, LLC; 52: Bridgeman Art Library/Art Gallery of New South Wales, Sydney, Australia © Kurt Schwitters. Licensed by DACS 2006; 56: © Jacob Jongert. Licensed by DACS 2006; 60: Bauhaus-Archiv Berlin, photography: Atelier Schneider; 62, 64: Merrill C. Berman Collection, photography: Jim Frank; 68: Bridgeman Art Library/Private Collection, Giraudon © Hannah Höch. Licensed by DACS 2006; 72: Museum of Modern Art, New York/Scala, Florence © Filippo Tommaso Marinetti. Licensed by DACS 2006; 74: Courtesy The Depero Archive © Fortunato Depero. Licensed by DACS 2006; 80, 82: Robert Opie Collection; 86: Robert Opie Collection © 1926 Condé Nast Publications. Reprinted by permission. All rights reserved; 88: Museum of Modern Art, New York/Scala, Florence; 90: akg images; 94t: Corbis/Swim Ink 2, LLC © Transport for London; 94b: Courtesy and © Transport for London; 96: Science & Society Picture Library/NRM - Pictorial Collection; 107, 112: Robert Opie Collection; 116: Library of Congress, Washington, DC © Max Bill. Licensed by DACS 2006; 121: Robert Opie Collection; 126: Estate of Abram Games; 128: Library of Congress, Washington, DC; 132: Courtesy Blue Note Records; 136: Courtesy Karl Lundgren; 137: Courtesy Martin Sharp; 138: Robert Opie Collection; 144: Robert Opie Collection, courtesy Martin Sharp; 148: Robert Opie Collection; 150: Milton Glaser; 152: The Residents, *Diskomo*, courtesy of The Cryptic Corporation; 155: Courtesy Neville Brody; 156: International Institute of Social History, Amsterdam © Ospaal; 158: Courtesy of The Herb Lubalin Study Center of Design and Typography at The Cooper Union School of Art; 160: Museum für Gesaltung Zürich, Poster Collection. Photography by Franz Xaver Jaggy; 162: Courtesy Takenobu Igarashi; 164: Jamie Reid - www.jamiereid.uk.net; 166: Courtesy Neville Brody.

All other images from private collections.

Every effort has been made to contact copyright holders. If any omissions have been made, the publishers would be grateful for notification so that future reprints may be amended.